Great Knits

Texture and Color Techniques

from **Threads**

Great Knits

Texture and Color Techniques

from *Threads*

The Taunton Press

Cover and back-cover photos: Susan Kahn

Taunton
BOOKS & VIDEOS
for fellow enthusiasts

First printing: 1995
Printed in the United States of America

A Threads Book

Threads® is a trademark of The Taunton Press, Inc.,
registered in the U.S. Patent and Trademark Office.

The Taunton Press
63 South Main Street
P.O. Box 5506
Newtown, CT 06470-5506

Library of Congress Cataloging-in-Publication Data

Great knits : texture and color techniques / from Threads.
    p. cm.
   "A Threads book" — T.p. verso
   Includes index.
   ISBN 1-56158-103-8
   1. Knitting. 2. Sweaters. I. Threads magazine.
TT680.G73 1995   95-10422
 746.43'20432 — dc20   CIP

Contents

Introduction

ou've got the knitting basics down and now you're ready to expand your repertoire. Here, from the pages of *Threads* magazine, you'll find the inspiration and techniques you need.

Take your favorite sweater pattern and create an entirely new look. Add subtle shading to a Fair Isle design. Create a graphic beauty one block at a time. Choose two colors you love and knit a warm, reversible sweater. Embellish a sweater with geometric designs.

Or create interest with texture. Experiment with new ways to build a fabric. Knit in a new direction. Drop stitches and weave into open spaces. You can even create a fabric from the center out.

With *Great Knits*, you'll also learn basic techniques that will benefit every garment you knit. You'll find advice on what yarns and needles work best, how to make gauge swatches, and how to shape and finish the garment. But best of all, you'll create sweaters that you'll wear and love for years.

Suzanne LaRosa, publisher

Knit One, Weave Two

Dropped stitches create ideal spaces to weave color into your knitting

Linda M. McGurn

Combining woven panels in your knitting allows you to create unusual tweedlike fabrics, like that in this sweater jacket.

many knitters, I'm sure, long for a technique that allows them to knit colorful fabrics without the messiness of bobbins or the tangle of yarn floats on the back of the fabric. Well, I've found one, and it offers wonderful possibilities for design. It works exceptionally well for creating plaids and tweedlike effects (see my sweater jacket in the photo on the facing page) and is terrific for knitting oversize garments like jackets, coats, and men's sweaters. It helps stabilize these garments vertically and reduces the bulk and weight they would have if they were entirely knitted. It's also a great way to use up leftover yarn from other projects. So, what is this miracle technique? It's actually not purely a knitting technique, but rather needle weaving combined with knitting.

I came across the idea for mixing knitting and weaving when a friend asked me to copy a favorite machine-knit sweater with lots of ladderlike openwork. At first, I was stumped by the openwork, but then I realized it was made by simply dropping stitches from the knitting needle, creating a perfect ladder (see *Threads* No. 52, pp. 20-21). As I was knitting the sweater, a light bulb flashed on: Dropping stitches would create an ideal warp for needle weaving. Eureka!

Needle-weaving technique
Needle weaving is simple and requires only a few tools (see the list of supplies on p. 11). As shown on pp. 10-11, it involves first knitting a piece of fabric in stockinette stitch, then transferring all the stitches of the completed knitting onto a 24-in. circular needle (to give you room to work) instead of binding them off. A warp is made for weaving by dropping a given number of stitches, which unravel along the entire length of the knitting. The warp is then pinned to a flat surface and filled by weaving lengths of yarn (threaded into a tapestry needle) through it.

You can use whatever weaving pattern you like (basketweave, twill, etc.), but I find that plain weave (over one, under one) works well to give me a variety of effects. Whatever pattern you use, be sure not to pack the warp too tightly or the woven sections will be stiff and won't drape like the rest of the knitted fabric.

Gauge
To incorporate needle weaving into your knitted projects, you'll need to make two separate gauge swatches: one of the stockinette knitting before you've dropped stitches and another of the woven panels worked on the dropped-stitch warp. Your stockinette gauge should be approximately 4 in. square. The woven gauge should be taken across the full width of a completed woven panel. For the woven gauge, simply figure out how many stitches you've dropped and how wide a warp—and consequently woven section—the dropped stitches yield. After you've tried the technique a few times, you may find that you can take the woven gauge directly from the outstretched, unwoven warp. But, if you're working with a plaid or an unusual weave pattern, always take the woven gauge from a completed woven panel.

You'll find that dropping a stitch yields a warp between about ½ and 1 in. wide, depending on your needle size and yarn weight. Because dropping stitches adds width, the initial knitted piece will be narrower than the finished piece with woven panels; and the more woven panels, the wider the finished piece.

Designing a garment
The entire process of making a garment with this technique takes from a couple of days to a week or so, depending on how complex your garment is, how many woven panels it has, and, of course, how much time you're able to spend on it every day. If you knit the basic stockinette fabric by machine rather than by hand, you'll considerably speed up the process.

After much experimentation with this technique, I've decided that I like to design and work a rectangle or square of knitted/woven fabric and then cut the completed fabric to the shapes I need for my garment. To plot a design in a fabric rectangle using this technique, start with the width of the garment you want to make. Then make a diagram like the sample shown below, showing all the knitted and woven panels you plan. Note on the diagram the width of each knitted and woven panel and the number of stitches needed or the number to be dropped to yield this width.

I suggest starting your garment design at center front, deciding first if you want knitting or weaving down the middle, then working out the design on either side. (This is important even when you're plotting a plaid.) If you've designed from the center out and, by chance, your gauge turns out to be off in the actual piece, this

---

Planning a knit/woven fabric

Here's how to plan a sample piece of fabric, using your knitting and weaving gauge swatches.

No. of stitches needed	7 K	1 W	7 K		3 W		7 K	1 W	7 K	=33 sts

No. of finished inches	1½	1	1½		3		1½	1	1½	= 11 in.

K = knitted sts
W = woven panel worked on no. of dropped sts indicated.

Gauges:
Stockinette gauge = 5 sts/in.
Woven gauge = 1 dropped st/1 in.; 3 dropped sts/3 in.

1. *Figure out the knitted and woven gauges.*
2. *Decide where to insert woven panels in knitting.*
3. *Establish width of each knitted and woven panel and number of stitches needed to yield that width.*
4. *Calculate overall width of fabric and total number of stitches needed.*

arrangement allows you to cut off the side edges without affecting the center of your design.

If you plan a woven panel at an edge of your fabric, add a knit stitch to that edge to make your seam. If two abutting edges end in woven panels, add a knit stitch to each edge.

Shaping and finishing a garment

Once my fabric is finished, I draw the shapes of the garment pieces directly on the fabric with chalk or small dots of typing correction fluid, which works well and flakes off easily when I'm done. Then, with the machine, I straight-stitch one row and zigzag a second row around the shapes of my garment pieces, cut out the shapes, and sew them together at the shoulders and side seams. I pick up stitches around the neck, wrists, and bottom edge of the body, including in the woven areas, and knit regular ribbing to complete the garment. □

Linda M. McGurn is a fiber artist in South Barrington, IL, who specializes in knit/woven garments and gives workshops on the technique.

Using needle weaving in your knitting reduces the weight and bulk produced by traditional colorwork techniques, enabling you to create oversize garments like this lined coat.

Creating knit/woven fabric

The process of creating a knit/woven fabric is a simple one that involves dropping stitches from stockinette fabric and needle-weaving in the resulting ladder warp. As shown below, the process produces fabrics distinctly different from the initial stockinette fabrics from which they emerge.

The knit/woven fabric this technique produces is dramatically different from and considerably wider than the 10-in.-wide base stockinette fabric from which it's made (at left in the photo). In the finished 24½-in.-wide fabric, the knitted stripes remain only as very narrow bands between the woven plaid panels.

1 Knit stockinette fabric and drop stitches for weaving: After completing the base stockinette fabric, transfer all stitches to a 24-in. circular needle. Working from the diagram you've plotted after establishing your gauges (see the drawing on p. 9), drop the required number of stitches at the appropriate points in the fabric the full length of the knitting. Dropping a single stitch in single-ply, sportweight yarn yields almost 1 in. of warp thread. The more stitches you drop, the wider the warp, as you can see in the photo below, in which three stitches are being dropped.

2 Straighten and secure the warp yarns: Pin the fabric on each side of the warp to a piece of fiberboard covered with graph paper, stretching the yarns straight but not taut. Thread a length of yarn into a tapestry needle and weave the full length of the warp, as shown at left. Start a new length of yarn at each end of the weaving, and leave yarn tails 1 or 2 in. long at the top and bottom of the fabric. (Weaving with a single, continuous length of yarn is unwieldy and also tends to pull in the top and bottom of the warp.)

3 Comb the woven strands of yarn in the warp: Just as weavers use a beater to pack the newly woven weft yarns, use a wide-tooth comb to straighten and fill the warp, as shown at right. But don't pack the yarn too tightly, or the fabric will be stiff.

Supplies for weaving knits

- 24-in. circular knitting needle
- A piece of ½-in.-thick wood-fiber ceiling panel (available in building-supply stores) 2 to 4 in. longer and wider than the warp you're going to weave. Or you could use a blocking board, foamcore board, or any flat, rigid surface into which you can pin.
- Wide masking tape to cover the cut edges of the fiberboard and keep the knitting from snagging (I also cover the board with graph paper—hard to see in the photo above—to use as a guide for straightening the warp.)
- 1½-in.-long quilting pins (available at craft- and sewing-supply stores). Don't use T-pins, which catch the yarn.
- A wide-tooth comb or hair pick to tamp the woven threads
- A yarn darner or tapestry needle with blunt point and extra-large eye to weave yarn through warp

4 Finish the fabric edges: Instead of weaving each yarn tail into the back of the woven section, which makes the fabric too thick and doesn't work well with slippery yarns, finish the edges with a sewing machine. First use a wide-tooth comb to tamp the end rows and make them as even as possible. Then comb the yarn tails straight and iron them lightly. Move the fabric to the sewing machine, neatly rearrange the yarns tails, and, with the machine set to its longest stitch length, straight-stitch one row the full length of the fabric's edge over both the knitted and woven panels. Set the machine for a medium zigzag stitch, zigzag one row the full length of the edge, and trim the remaining ends to about ⅛ in. Repeat the procedure on the fabric's other long edge. Then shape and finish the garment as explained on the facing page.

Sweaters Piece by Piece

Working without a gauge, you can knit in all directions to create a unique fabric

by Natalina Carbone

Perhaps, like me, you're a long-time knitter who finds that traditional knitting is a bit, well, boring. For starters, there's the limitation of working across rows. And while you can knit in patterns and images, there is always something inherently geometric about the finished product. Maybe, like me, you're longing for something more fluid, more creative.

I had just about given up on knitting as a creative process when I came across a book entitled *Wool'n Magic* by Jan Messent (Kent, England: Search Press Ltd., 1989), which first got me thinking in terms of knitting fabrics, rather than sweaters. I started with some of the techniques described by Messent and kept experimenting.

The result is what I call *free-style knitting*. Combining knitting with ideas from quilting, collage, and textile design, the object is not to knit a sweater, but to make fabric that you then turn into a garment. You knit small segments in all directions, with the emphasis on color, yarn texture, and the way the two work together to form a fabric.

To do free-style knitting, you can forget much that you've already learned, although you will be using familiar stitches and equipment. You'll use standard knitting needles to do basic knit and purl stitches. You'll cast stitches on and off and pick up stitches with a crochet hook. But you will not worry about tension, gauge, dropped stitches, following instructions, or even buying yarn in matching dye lots. You work on lap-size pieces, which you'll sew or crochet together only at the end. You won't have to worry about making mistakes, because it's not possible to make a mistake.

Getting started

When planning a garment in free-style knitting, it's best to keep the shape as simple as possible, so that the emphasis will be on the fabric. Whether you want to make a cardigan, pullover, or dress, begin by selecting a style, from either a knitting pattern or a simple commercial sewing pattern. For many of my garments, squares and rectangles form the front, back, and sleeves. Using the measurements from the knitting diagram or the pattern pieces themselves, make a flat pattern from medium- to heavyweight nonwoven interfacing fabric, such as Pellon stabilizer, which will be the template for assembling the knitted pieces into the shape of the garment. To eliminate as many seams as possible, sew the interfacing sections together at the shoulders or side seams to make a large, flat template.

Selecting yarns and needles

After you've decided on the garment shape, pick out a color scheme. Think about the look you want to achieve. Perhaps you'd like something light and springlike, as in the lavender and white sweater in the photo on the facing page. Maybe bold and colorful is more to your taste. My first free-style sweater, for example, was inspired by autumn foliage, and was comprised of browns, yellows, greens, and reds I saw in the trees. Inspiration may simply come from a trip to a wonderful yarn store.

Gather together yarns in the colors you have chosen in as many different weights and textures as you can find. Choose anything that catches your eye—wools, synthetics, metallics, silks, cottons. The more variety of yarns you have, the better, because they give the fabric texture. Don't worry about compatibility, since the various materials used in small segments will blend together.

For needles, I prefer knitting with short double-pointed ones that are easy to maneuver, but you can also use regular needles. The size needle you choose depends on the look you want. I used size 7 needles for the lavender and white sweater, because the yarns are fairly fine and I wanted a firm fabric. Knitting the same yarns with a size 10 would give a looser, lacier effect. The garment will hold its shape no matter what size needles you use, because all the small cast-on and -off edges worked in different directions give the fabric stability.

Beginning to knit

Start by casting on a few stitches with one color of yarn and knit a few rows. The number of stitches in a segment can range from six to twelve; many short segments will result in a heavier and more varied fabric (the extra cast-on and -off rows add weight), while longer segments will result in a fabric that's lighter, with larger blocks of color.

I prefer stockinette stitch (knit a row, then purl a row), because I like the way it drapes. You can knit every row, but the resulting garter stitch makes the fabric heavier and less fluid. I've experimented with patterns and stitches such as seed, cables, and lace patterns, but the free-style technique has so much color and texture that the fancier stitches can get lost.

Keep working until you have a small, roughly square piece, then cast off. It doesn't

Making stable, textured fabric, as in the sweater on the facing page, requires no written pattern, and uses plenty of leftover yarns.

From *Threads* magazine (June 1994) 53:52-55

*Cast off with a crochet hook
in the place of the right-hand
knitting needle: Knit two
stitches, then pull the second
one through the first with the
crochet hook. Repeat to the
end, then cut the yarn, and
pull it through the last stitch.*

*Pick up stitches along a
knitted edge by holding the
yarn behind the work,
inserting a crochet hook
(shown), and pulling up a
loop. Repeat for the number
of stitches desired, then knit
them off the hook with a
knitting needle.*

*To weave pieces of knitting
together: Thread yarn on a
blunt needle, and pick up a
stitch on the edge of one
side, then a stitch on the
opposite edge, pulling to butt
edges together without
creating a ridge. Continue to
alternate edges, turning
corners where necessary.*

matter whether you end with a knit or purl row. I cast off by holding a knitting needle in my left hand and a hook in my right, then knitting a stitch with the crochet hook (even on the purl side), knitting the next stitch, then pulling it through the first one with the crochet hook, as shown in the top photo at left. Repeat to the end of the row, cut the yarn a few inches away, then pull the tail through the last stitch.

Choose a second yarn and, using the crochet hook, pick up some stitches along one edge of the piece, as shown at left center. To make the fabric interesting and avoid a geometric look, don't pick up all the stitches on a side. Try picking up half the stitches on one side plus a few from another edge around a corner. Then knit the stitches onto a knitting needle.

When choosing the second yarn, keep in mind the overall effect you want. For a smooth, harmonious fabric, you can use a yarn in the same or similar color, but in a completely different texture. Or you may want more color contrast throughout the fabric. For one sweater, I used a palette of eight distinct colors, with every segment a different color from the adjacent one.

I like to work so that the fabric has a right and wrong side, with knit stitches on one side and purl on the other, but this is a matter of personal preference. Mixing knit and purl segments on the right side will give the fabric more texture.

After knitting the second segment for a while, cast off again. Then pick up some stitches on another edge of the original segment, perhaps including some stitches from the segment you just added. Using a third yarn, knit another segment onto the piece.

As you add segments, you will have yarn ends hanging where you cast off and join new fibers. I suggest working each end into the piece as you go along by either knitting it with the next stitches, picking stitches up under and over the end to weave it in, or sewing it in as you go along. By taking care of the yarn tails as you work, you won't have to deal with all of them at once.

Continue adding segments around the edges of the piece until you have a patchwork about 4 in. across. This size is manageable, flexible, and easy to assemble.

When you have one patchwork piece finished, start another. You can choose a different color family from your yarn palette or use the same yarns you worked with on the first piece. Either way, no two patchwork pieces will be alike, since you are working without specific instructions.

You can easily add beads to a piece by threading the beads on a strand of silk thread that blends with the yarn, then knitting the beaded thread right along with the yarn. Push a bead up next to the needle where you want it, and knit to catch the bead in place.

Assembling the pieces

When you've finished a dozen or so pieces, you can start making them into a fabric. With safety pins, attach the pieces to the flat Pellon template, fitting them together as you would assemble a jigsaw puzzle. You'll be surprised at how well the pieces fit together; don't worry if the edges don't match exactly, because you'll deal with this later.

The fabric is starting to grow to fit the pattern. As you produce more pieces and add them to the fabric, an overall design emerges. Feel free to move pieces around and knit more of some colors. You may even decide to go off in a different direction from the one you began, or add a color or texture that you hadn't originally planned. One of the most interesting aspects of this technique is learning how colors work together. If you want a color you don't have, try knitting with more than one strand of yarn at a time to blend a new color.

When you're happy with the way the pieces look, start fastening them together. You can thread a blunt tapestry needle with fine yarn and weave the pieces together, picking up one stitch at a time and alternating edges, as shown at bottom on the facing page. You can also crochet the pieces together, but I suggest working from the right side so you can see how the pieces look. As you sew, stretch, pull, push, gather, or tuck the pieces—whatever is necessary to make the edges meet. The fabric will have little hills and valleys but won't lose its basically flat nature.

If you have a hole in the fabric that you can't fill by pushing and pulling pieces together, knit a small patch the same size and shape as the empty space, and sew it in place.

It's not necessary for all of your patches to be knit. You can integrate wovens, leather, needlework pieces, crocheted pieces, or lace. Or you can make a sweater body from free-style knit pieces, and sleeves from woven fabric, Ultrasuede, or plain hand or machine knitting.

At the sleeve and side edges, you don't have to create straight seams. You can simply join them the way you have joined other pieces—stretching and tucking the edges to fit, and weaving them together. One easy way to join without obvious seams is to put the template (with the fabric pinned to it) on a dress form and work in the round, building the fabric from front to back and down the sleeves, as shown below.

Finishing

When you have completed the fabric, which is now in the form of a garment, remove any remaining safety pins and the underlying template. Add finishing details, but keep them simple—perhaps a collar, ribbing around the cuffs and bottom, and front bands and buttons for a cardigan. You can either pick up stitches along the edges and knit ribbings and bands, or knit them separately and sew them on. The ribbing can be a single layer for a lighter fabric or a double layer for a heavier one, such as for a jacket. I usually stick with one color for these borders, since the fabric is complex. If you are making a coat or jacket, you may want to add a lining.

A note about care of the fabric: It's fine to hand wash the garment, even if some of the yarn wrappers recommend dry-cleaning. One fiber may stretch, while another may shrink a bit, so they tend to balance each other, and the garment will hold its shape.

You can use free-style knitting for hats, pillows, or even bedspreads. Knitted patches can become appliqué sections for plain sweaters or jackets. You can even cut the knitted fabric to shape a neckline, machine stitching first to minimize raveling. Feel free to explore—let your imagination be your guide. □

Natalina Carbone teaches workshops and designs one-of-a-kind knitwear in Milwaukie, OR. She's currently working on integrating computer art with free-style knitting.

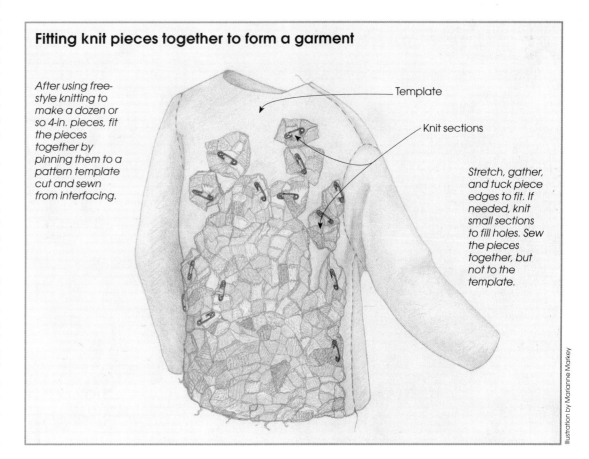

Fitting knit pieces together to form a garment

After using free-style knitting to make a dozen or so 4-in. pieces, fit the pieces together by pinning them to a pattern template cut and sewn from interfacing.

Template

Knit sections

Stretch, gather, and tuck piece edges to fit. If needed, knit small sections to fill holes. Sew the pieces together, but not to the template.

Swatches for Sweaters

Your knitted sample can tell you a lot more about your design than just the gauge

by Deborah Newton

When a knitter asks me what I've found most helpful for designing knitwear, I always say swatching. Knitting a swatch, or small piece of test fabric, is the best way to solidify a vague design idea into something tangible to look at and feel. I can't imagine designing a sweater without this crucial first step.

The swatching process helps you choose the best needle size and establish the gauge (number of stitches and rows per inch) for your fabric. It also allows you to experiment with pattern and color and see the weight and drape of a fabric before plunging into a project. Like most knitters, I used to swatch only to experiment with yarns, patterns, and design ideas, but now I like to create a swatch that, when possible, becomes part of my design.

Starting points for swatching

I usually have at least a vague idea of what I want to swatch. I may want to explore a particular yarn, stitch pattern, or design idea—or maybe all three things at once. If you're new to swatching, keep things simple. Begin with a yarn or a pattern, but don't try juggling ideas until you gain more experience.

Try to keep a very loose grip on any preconceived ideas since the swatch will often surprise you—whether with delightful or frustrating results. The process is such that you'll often need to stop in midstream to reconsider your materials and goals. See what happens as you swatch, then change course accordingly.

Starting with yarn—If yarn is your starting point, get out your pattern dictionaries and try several patterns to find the one that looks best with your yarn. Generally the more textured the yarn, the simpler the pattern stitch should be. And the lighter the color, the better the yarn will show off patterning. When swatching with more than one color, try first knitting simple stripes to test color combinations, then work more complex patterns with the combinations you like.

Starting with a pattern stitch—If you start with a stitch pattern, or a family of stitches, like lace, don't settle for the first yarn you try unless it really enhances your pattern. Swatch with several yarns of different weights and textures to find what best suits your stitch.

When testing several stitches, you can work separate swatches for each, a long

Testing stitch patterns: When you've selected a yarn, swatching helps you find complementary patterns.

Testing color combinations: The lapel-shaped swatch at left shows gauge, color sequences, and edge trims and could be added to a sweater as a collar.

From *Threads* magazine (August 1994) 54:60-61

swatch testing one pattern after another, or a wide swatch testing patterns side by side. Arranging patterns vertically allows you to see how one pattern combines with another and how best to separate them. Arranging them horizontally works well for testing cabled patterns in classic Aran style but requires planning at the cast-on stage to accommodate all the patterns as well as the stitches needed to separate the patterns.

Starting with a garment shape or detail—If you begin with a particular garment shape or detail, experiment with various yarns and patterns, starting simple and working up to more complex, before settling on what's most effective. Use the swatch to test garment details you have in mind; you may even want to shape the swatch to test a certain garment section.

Making a useful swatch

Think about the swatch's size, shape, and edges before casting on. The most useful swatch measures at least 6 to 8 in. square. Generally speaking, the heavier the yarn, the larger the swatch should be to give you a feel for the finished fabric. Take an educated guess about your yarn and cast on enough stitches to yield 6 to 8 in. in width. For a worsted yarn yielding 5 sts/ in., for example, I cast on 30 to 40 stitches. If I'm knitting a pattern that repeats, I cast on an even multiple within this stitch range.

I always add a garter or stockinette stitch or two to both sides of the swatch to help isolate the pattern and keep the swatch edges flat. Doing this also makes it easier to pick up stitches along the edge and seam the swatch if it is later used in the garment (see "Using your swatch" at right).

Starting or ending your swatch with ribbing or another edging will give you an idea of how these finishes will look on the sweater. To check the look of a cardigan front

band, pick up stitches and knit a band along a side edge.

Finally, you can use your swatch to test finishing and blocking techniques. For example, I steam pure wool or mohair swatches to full the fibers slightly and stabilize the fabric. And I stretch or pull swatches made of stretchy yarns like rayon to simulate wear before measuring gauge (for more on preparing your swatch, see "An Accurate Knitting Gauge Made Easy" in *Threads* No. 51, pp. 59-61).

Using your swatch

After completing a swatch, think about how to apply what you've learned to planning your garment. Try posing a few questions: Which patterns in the swatch are the most successful? Does the swatch tell you all you need to know, or should you work another one to test additional ideas and questions? If the fabric is stiff, which garment shape will best use this feature? And so on.

In addition to using the ideas you get from a swatch, you can use the actual swatch in your garment. For example, the swatch might make a good inside or outside pocket. A pair of rectangular swatches could serve as fancy epaulets. A lengthened swatch might become a collar. Or by planning ahead, you can shape the swatch to become a certain part of the garment, as in my lapel swatch shown on the facing page.

Sometimes a swatch just doesn't fit your design. When this happens, make it into a small purse by adding a backing and a zipper, or use it for a doll's sweater. If you swatch only, as the patterns say, "to obtain the given gauge," rethink how this simple process can add to your designing pleasure and, with planning, become a useful component of your garment. □

Deborah Newton is a knitwear designer and a contributing editor to Threads.

Testing elements of a design: This denim-jacket-inspired swatch, which could be used as a pocket, includes edgings, yoke detail, and embroidery that mimics the contrasting seaming on classic blue jeans.

Corrugated Knitting

Pull in those floats for a sweater that's warm and toasty

by Molly Gordon

my best friend in all the world once knit me a pair of slippers. They were carmine and slate, knit in blocks of five stitches by four rows. At each color change she pulled the yarn taut—just the opposite of the stranding instructions for Fair Isle—and the result was a ridged fabric that was exceptionally stretchy and warm.

Inspired by down vests, I used the technique to knit several vests in corrugated fabric. I also experimented with corrugated torsos and stockinette sleeves.

Characteristics of corrugated fabric

The heat-trapping ability of the corrugated ridges crossed by strands of yarn is considerable, making the fabric extremely warm. It is also bulky, although in very close fitting garments the bulk will be minimized as the ridges stretch around the body. The vertical lines of the ridges can also offset the bulkiness. Knit in two-colored stripes, the fabric will visually elongate the figure of the wearer. Knit in a two- (or more) colored checkerboard, this elongation is less pronounced.

Corrugated fabric is heavy. The "Op Art" jacket shown on the facing page (a close-fitting size 6/8) weighs 28 ounces. A noncorrugated jacket in the same yarn would weigh about 20 ounces.

Corrugated fabric is more elastic across its width than along its length, although the fabric tends to become narrower and denser as the length of the knitted piece increases. You will count fewer stitches per inch in a swatch that is 40 stitches wide by 16 rows long than you will in a swatch that's 40 stitches by 64 rows because the stranding condenses the fabric more in the longer swatch. Both of the swatches can be stretched to the same width, but you really need to judge the fabric gauge in its relaxed state. If you want to make sure that you have plenty of ease in a corrugated jacket, you should make a large gauge swatch—at least 5 by 10 inches.

What can you do with it?

Corrugated fabric is appropriate wherever warmth is desirable and bulk is not a problem. The slippers which started my

Thick, stretchy, and delightfully warm, this unusual jacket is simple to make. It's adapted from your favorite set-in sleeve pattern using directions given in the article. You knit it in stockinette stitch, and make the ridges as you change the colors. (Photos by Susan Kahn)

romance with corrugations were ideal. The cushiony bulk provided protection from cold floors, and the elastic fabric hugged my feet. The rolled edge, which occurs naturally in stockinette corrugated fabric, made a neat finish at the vamp without hemming or ribbing.

Thick, warm corrugation is very well suited for cold weather outerwear. A loose-fitting corrugated jacket could replace a traditional parka; a vest over a polypropylene turtleneck may be all you need for cross-country skiing; and in arctic conditions, the vest can be layered under a parka. Because the ridges are backed by closely crossed strands of yarn, as you can see in the photo at right, this fabric offers more protection from the wind than do most knits.

Sometimes the efficient insulation of corrugated fabric is *too* warm. Although I knitted a pullover vest for my husband to ski in, I prefer to wear cardigan styles with zippers. By opening and closing a zipper, I can control ventilation and moderate heat, so I often use zippers in my vests and jackets.

Choosing a pattern

For your first corrugated garment, choose a simple set-in sleeve jacket or vest pattern. Avoid fussy details; the fabric will be the highlight of your sweater. A crew or turtleneck works best. Set-in sleeve styles work better than dropped-shoulder styles for corrugated knits. The bulky fabric will bunch uncomfortably and unattractively at the underarm of styles with dropped shoulders.

Finding the right yarn

This is the fun part! Corrugated knitting transforms any yarn into an exciting fabric. Corrugated fabric requires approximately 40 percent more yarn per garment than plain stockinette, so it's wise to consider your fiber and color choices carefully before investing in yarn. For your first project, choose two compatible colors. Take the yardage required by your chosen pattern, add 40 percent, and divide by two. That gives you the approximate yardage you will need for each yarn. Buy an extra ball or skein of the color you'll use for collar and cuffs.

Washable wool and wool blends are ideal fibers for corrugated knitting. They are resilient, and the more resilient the yarn, the more pronounced the corrugations. Because it is a natural fiber, wool breathes better than synthetic fibers. Synthetics can make the already toasty corrugated fabric uncomfortably warm.

Choose yarns with plenty of twist. Loosely twisted yarns can fray when you

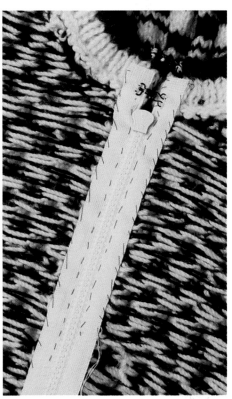

The insulating quality of ridges backed by crossing yarns gives corrugated sweaters exceptional warmth. Stitching the zipper on both sides of the tape as shown is a neat, secure way to attach it.

pull the strands taut at color changes. To check for both twist and resilience, stretch about 4 in. of yarn gently. If it stretches a little and recovers without shredding, the yarn will probably be fine.

Swatching

It is essential to make swatches before you adapt a pattern for corrugated knitting. Only by knitting a generous swatch can you assess the characteristics of this fabric in a given yarn.

Ribbing—Start your gauge swatches with ribbing. Use needles specified in your pattern or choose a set two sizes smaller than the needles recommended by your yarn's manufacturer. Cast on at least 40 stitches in one color. Rib for two or three inches. K1, p1 or k2, p2 ribs both work well.

Increase row—This row will help you determine the proper proportion between the number of stitches in the ribbing and the number used in the corrugated section. In general, increase one stitch every other stitch across the last row of ribbing to obtain the number of stitches needed for the pattern fabric. I like to use a lifted increase, which adds a stitch almost invisibly (see *Threads* No. 39, p. 16).

Pattern stitch—For the nicest looking transition from rib to pattern stitch, knit the increase row in the colors and with the (larger) needles you plan to use for the pattern. Thus, your increase row is also row 1 of your corrugated pattern.

Tie the second color yarn around the main color at the edge, then knit groups of five stitches, alternating colors across the row. Purl the return row, keeping to the color changes of row 1. If you want a striped swatch, always use the same colors as you work from row to row. For a checkerboard pattern, switch the color order every four rows.

Use the swatching process to spur your creativity by working with several color combinations as the swatch progresses. If all your colors are in the same weight and type of yarn, your gauge will be as valid as if you had worked in only one or two colors. You then not only have gauge information, but also color and pattern possibilities to apply to your project.

Once you've chosen your pattern and have an accurate gauge, adjust the pattern directions. Use your swatch and the following guidelines to determine the number of stitches to cast on, appropriate increases, and shaping.

As a general rule, cast on and rib two-thirds the number of stitches needed for the corrugated pattern. If your corrugated swatch has a gauge of seven stitches to the inch and the sweater back needs to be 20 inches wide, you'll need 140 stitches across the back. If you multiply 140 by ⅔, you get 93.3 stitches. Round off and cast on 94 stitches for the ribbing.

Instead of rounding each row or stitch calculation up to the nearest stitch, as I normally do, I round corrugated knitting up or down by full color blocks. If I want a loose fit, and my math tells me I need 142 stitches, I will increase to 145 in a five-stitch, four-row pattern. For a closer fit, I'll use 140. I like to bind off on a knit row, so I round the row count by color block, too. The fabric is elastic enough that the difference isn't critical.

After you've calculated the stitches needed for your gauge, add one stitch at each side of each pattern piece for seaming. By wrapping the yarns before you come to this extra stitch, you can preserve the final ridge and still have one flat stitch on each edge for a seam allowance. Pick up the yarn you're using under the yarn dropped at the end of the previous color block, and wrap the working yarn over between the fifth and sixth stitches at the end of each row. I experimented with a narrower channel at the front edges of the "Op Art" jacket. The final ridge at the front edges is four stitches wide including the edge stitch. This rolls very neatly into the zipper tape.

Swatch some slippers—Once you've established the right proportions for your ribbing and pattern stitches, you can make swatches without ribbing. Make swatches five to seven inches wide and about three inches longer than your foot. Don't bind off. Thread the yarn through the last row, and pull tight for the toe of the slipper. Fold the swatch and seam the cast-on edge for the heel. Sew the sides together for two or three inches from the toe, and you're done.

Designs in corrugated knitting

To make the "Op Art" jacket, I knit in stockinette, alternating yarns every five stitches. You can vary the depth of the ridges. Alternate yarns every three stitches for a fine-ribbed effect. Alternate every eight and get very deep ribs. The five-stitch alternation works nicely for clothing and, in most yarns, gives a rea-sonably square checkerboard effect when yarn selections are reversed every four rows. The five-stitch and four-row repeat also makes for rapid calculation of stitch and row quantities.

Color corrugations—Corrugated knitting invites color work. By changing colors every four rows, you can transform your bargain yarns and remainders into a crazy checkerboard. Use two colors consistently and you'll get vertical stripes. Closely allied colors will give a heathery effect; contrasting colors, a more vivid result. The swatch in the photo on the facing page shows some of the possibilities. You may even work a solid-color corrugated piece by working with two balls of the same yarn.

Adventurous knitters may use more than two colors in a row. To maintain regular puckering of the fabric, be sure to wrap a new color as shown in the photos below. Of course, you might choose to make a fabric with random puckering.

Shaping

Increase and decrease at the outer edge of your garment piece when shaping sleeves, armscyes, and necklines. I make my increases in the very first and last stitches, then sew my seams with mattress stitch (see *Threads* No. 35, p. 20), picking up every bar between stitches. Because you're working with more stitches in each row than normal, you'll find that you need to increase and decrease much more rapidly than you do in stockinette fabric.

For fitted sleeves, calculate the number of stitches you need at the top of the cuff. Subtract this from the number of stitches you need to knit the fullest part of the sleeve before you begin to bind off for the underarm. Using your swatch, de-

It's easy to add blocks of a third color and keep the fabric corrugations if you remember to wrap the third yarn color in the last stitch of the block, once removed. Pick up the working yarn (white) under the third-color yarn (red) on knit rows, as shown at *left. The photo at right shows what's happening on the wrong side. Notice how the red yarn was tied to the white exactly below the stitch where it's wrapped. Gordon drops the taupe yarn to corru-gate the taupe block by crossing it with the red yarn.*

termine the number of rows needed to knit from the top of the cuff to the underarm bind-off row.

For example (all horizontal measurements across slightly stretched fabric): My gauge is 25 stitches and 15 rows to 3 inches. The length from the top of the cuff to the underarm is 14½ inches or 72 rows. There are 75 stitches at the top of the cuff (after increasing from rib). The width at the underarm is 17½ inches or 145 stitches. The difference between 145 and 75 is 70 stitches. Increase 70 stitches overall, 35 stitches at each side of the sleeve, over 72 rows. You'll need to make your increases every other row, working the last two rows even before binding off for the underarm.

Calculate the decreases for the sleeve cap in the same manner.

Binding off

Two factors must be considered when you bind off corrugated fabric: the number of yarns you're using in a row and the corrugations. After much experimenting, I believe the neatest way to carry two or more yarns across a bound-off edge is to alternate the colors at every stitch until the bind-off is complete.

I decrease as I bind off to retain the corrugated effect at the very edge of the fabric. In general, knit one (k1), knit two together (k2tog), and pass the first stitch over the second stitch to bind off. K1 for the next bind-off stitch, k2tog for the third, and so on until you have removed the desired number of stitches.

In my black and white sample, I removed eight stitches at the underarm on the backs, fronts, and sleeves as follows: k1 (white), k2tog (black), bind off (pass first st over), k1 (white), bind off, k2tog (black), bind off, k1 (white), bind off, k2tog (black), bind off.

I have reduced the number of stitches by eight, but the bound-off edge is only five stitches long, preserving the corrugated effect. If you elect to bind off without decreasing, you will have to gather the edge of your sleeve cap to fit as you sew it into the armscye.

Finishing up

Concealing ends of yarn in corrugated fabric is a breeze. In addition to the many methods available for stockinette fabric, you can conceal the ends by pulling them through the channels between the face of the fabric and the crossed strands on the back.

The longer your pattern piece, the more your fabric will draw in from side to side, making your pattern piece seem longer than it will be when blocked.

Blocking the finished garment will offset this compression somewhat, but to make sure I don't get any surprises, I check often by measuring the fabric slightly stretched to see that I'm getting approximate blocked measurements.

I've inserted many zippers into sweaters by hand and by machine. I believe that hand sewing after careful pinning is the fastest and most certain way to a nice zipper. I sew the zipper on both sides of the zipper tape, as shown in the photo on p. 19. Block your garment before buying the zipper so you can choose the right length. A zipper that's a bit short is better than one a little long. Use hooks and eyes to make a neat closure at the top.

I avoid button bands on corrugated knits because the horizontal stretch tends to make bands pucker and pull.

You can vary the look and warmth of your corrugated garments by using a different stitch pattern for the sleeves. Plain stockinette is very effective. You might knit the sleeves in horizontal stripes to contrast with vertical corrugations in the sweater body. A basketweave stitch can mirror a checkerboard colorway. I've also made sleeves with a bulky cable up the center with reverse stockinette background. The cable and the background were each knit in one of the colors of the striped body. □

Molly Gordon designs and knits sweaters and accessories in her studio on Bainbridge Island, WA. She sells her work under her Mollycoddles label at major craft fairs and at fine specialty shops.

Heathery, vivid, or striped: *Make your gauge swatch do double duty by experimenting with colors. Changing the values changes the look of the fabric. Molly's colorful checkerboard sweater in leftover yarns shows the possibilities.*

Designing Knit Fabrics

A ready-to-wear sweater sparks ideas
for combining strips diagonally

by Deborah Newton

From *Threads* magazine (April 1994) 52:58-61

*a*s a knitwear designer, I'm always on the lookout for an unusual knitted garment that can serve as a springboard for my own designs. I don't necessarily want to copy another piece, but instead let its strong features filter into and inspire my own work. A perfect example is the late 1970s Issey Miyake sweater I saw recently, shown in the photo on p. 24. Made entirely of 2-in.-wide knitted strips sewn together to lie diagonally across the body, the sweater sent me right home to start experimenting with some new fabrics.

Knitting samples (also called design swatches) is an important part of the design process and a quick, low-risk way to experiment with yarns, color, and texture. You can always start by duplicating what you've seen, but you'll quickly discover other possibilities when you vary the arrangement of colors and textures, among other characteristics. Here's how I go about experimenting with samples using diagonal strips.

Designing diagonal strips

After analyzing a source of ideas, such as the Miyake sweater, I usually identify the elements that strongly affect the appearance of the garment's fabric. These elements include yarn texture, color, stitch pattern, and, in this case, the strip width. Each element has many possible variations, as you'll see.

Choosing yarns—Working in narrow strips is perfect for those knitters who have a surplus of leftover yarns in any weight, texture, or color. You can mix yarns with different fiber contents, although I prefer fibers that can be steamed lightly for a finished look, especially around the seams.

The look of the yarn strand itself creates a texture in the fabric. For example, in stockinette stitch, a smooth yarn generally produces a smooth fabric, while a slubbed, hairy, or unusual plied yarn provides a rougher texture. You might want to alternate matte textures with shiny or slick yarns. Mixing yarns of different fibers and twists gives the fabric variety in texture and weight. In my swatch shown on p. 25, I used many cottons and synthetics, including ribbon, as well as slubbed, smooth, and shiny yarns.

To keep the width of my strips uniform from start to finish, I decided to stay with yarns of the same or similar weight. If you use different weights of yarn within the same strip, the strip will have uneven, wavy edges. This creates an interesting effect if you alternate a heavy yarn with a lighter one in a regularly repeating pattern, then assemble the strips so that light and heavy squares match up checkerboard-style to create a flat, manageable fabric. Or if you want a wild, unpredictable fabric, try mixing yarns of different weights randomly within the strips, then let the uneven edges become part of the fabric.

Adding color—The simplest way to create interesting color within a strip is to choose a variegated yarn that changes color gradually when knit in a narrow width, as I did in the swatch on the facing page. I knit three identical strips, but because the yarn changes color differently in each strip, the assembled fabric has an interesting random color pattern.

When designing with more than one yarn, gather a variety of yarn shades that you think might work well together. Colors don't look the same in a fabric as they do in skeins, so knitting swatches helps to refine the color mix. I had fun making the swatch on p. 25, because I assembled about two dozen different yarns (my leftovers), then experimented to narrow them down to the nine that work best together. The final swatch includes yarns of many different textures and colors, all in soft pastels built around a sherbet-toned variegated viscose ribbon.

Knitting in texture—Instead of creating a lot of elaborate colorwork, you can introduce variety and interest in the strips by knitting with textured stitches. I knit an interesting swatch in natural cream and ivory yarns, with each strip in a slightly different shade and yarn texture, and alternated blocks of stockinette turned knit or purl side out with sections of knit/purl patterns such as seed stitch. You might try inserting a simple cable at points along a strip, or for the whole length of a strip. In a multicolored swatch, you can work each block of color in a different textured stitch. Wider strips have more stitches, making room for more intricate patterning.

Arranging the strips

Depending on how you arrange and sew the knit strips, you can create many different fabrics. You'll find that designing can occur as you knit. Try holding strips next to each other as you work to see what kind of effects are possible. Since the strips are small, you can easily rip out and reknit them to test an idea in progress.

You can also use paper and colored pencils to plan strip combinations. Draw diagonal strips and sketch areas of color, pattern, or texture based on some initial swatching. Working on paper is especially helpful when designing plaids or other challenging allover patterns.

For an evenly balanced fabric, knit strips that are all the same width (2- to 4-in. widths work well), as I've done in my swatches. If you want an irregular pattern with a more haphazard look, you can knit and combine strips of varied widths. Whether your design is simple or complicated, make the final sample at least three

One yarn, many colors: A variegated yarn knit in strips provides many color changes without switching yarns. This fabric sample is only one of many that can be generated by an idea from a designer's sweater.

A designer sweater offers a rich source of ideas

A late 1970s Issey Miyake sweater incorporates several unusual knitting ideas with a high level of order and symmetry. Nine colors repeat through the diagonal strips to form a soft plaid, with reversed seams adding surface texture.

A diagram of the Miyake sweater

Narrow strips of knitting placed on the diagonal, cleverly knit to size and assembled to form a complete sweater unit, result in an unusual garment. There are traditional seams at the inside of the sleeves only.

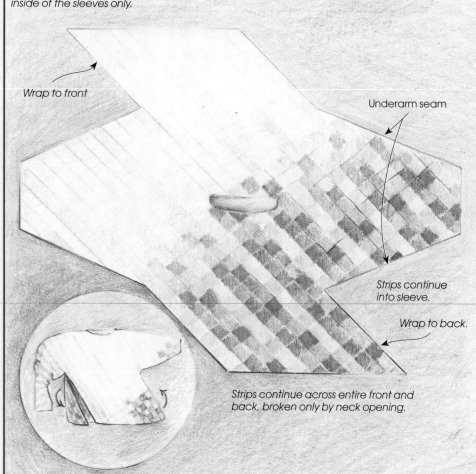

Wrap to front

Underarm seam

Strips continue into sleeve.

Wrap to back.

Strips continue across entire front and back, broken only by neck opening.

Garments from leading designers are ideal places to look for inspiration and fresh design ideas. Fortified with years of experience, plus the budget and staff to experiment until a piece is just right, many designers turn out garments chock full of interesting color, construction, and finishing techniques.

Issey Miyake has always been one of my favorite designers. Known as an innovator, he employs unusual fabrics and techniques, building them into uniquely shaped and detailed garments. Studying these designs never fails to lead me to new discoveries in my own work.

Like many Miyake designs, the beautiful sweater in the photo at left provoked both delight and puzzlement in me. In spite of my falling in love with the fabric, which was formed entirely of diagonally aligned strips knitted in a subtle array of colors, I couldn't quite figure out how the garment was assembled. At first I assumed that a large piece of strip fabric had been prepared, then the sweater cut out of the fabric and sewn together. But looking closer, I realized that the garment contains no cut edges and almost no seams aside from those between the strips.

Colors form a plaid

The sweater, which looks like a soft, muted handknit, is actually a wonder of order and symmetry. Nine colors of yarn form a subtle plaid, creating a repeated pattern of color and texture. The yarns are divided into three distinct color groups, each containing three yarns knitted into a repeated sequence of color in 2-in. squares. To make the fabric, these strips repeat so that the colors appear at regular intervals across the entire sweater.

The yarns all knit to about 5 sts/in. Some yarns are bulkier than others; the lightweight pale gray yarn forms open, weblike squares that contrast with other squares knit in heavier yarns, adding visual and textural interest.

Creating texture

Most of the squares in each strip show the nubby, purl side of stockinette as the right side. Occasionally, though, a square is worked with the smoother, knit side up, which creates a subtle variation in texture. These knit squares seem to occur randomly, but as you might expect in this orderly garment, they actually form a precise pattern. In each strip, every fourth square, then every fifth square, alternately, shows the knit side up. The sparse knit squares repeat in horizontal bands across areas of the sweater.

Sweater structure

On first glance, it looks as if the sweater is turned inside out, but this reversal is typical of Miyake's desire to present everything in a fresh, untraditional way. The strips, assembled with the seams on the right side to give texture, are carefully handsewn, apparently with a mattress stitch.

When I realized that the strips are arranged like a puzzle to form the sweater, I decided that whoever planned and designed this garment must love a challenge. The only seams are those of the strips themselves, plus two underarm sleeve seams, as shown in the diagram on the facing page. No side seams interrupt the body at all; there are only strips wrapping around the body from front to back, and some strips from the body wrap over the arm to form part of the sleeve. Each strip is a different length, depending on where it begins and ends in the sweater.

To create straight edges at the hems and neck opening, Miyake shaped the ends of each strip with partial rows so that the strips form a 45- to 50-degree angle with the hem. A row of crochet, worked in one of the yarns from the sweater body, finishes all the sweater's edges with a firm, stable accent of color. Okay, so we may not want to knit a sweater *this* complicated. But the wealth of ideas will be sneaking into my work for quite a while. — D.N.

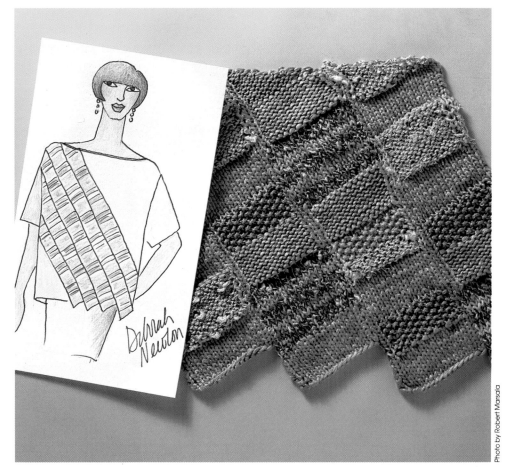

Photo by Robert Marsala

Mixing many yarns in a diagonal strip fabric gives a random, multicolor effect, even though the same stripe and texture patterns repeat throughout the swatch. Inset, a sketch of a summer sweater uses a few strips of the technique, including a zigzag lower edge formed from the square ends of the strips.

or four strips wide, so you'll have an idea of the overall effect and will see how the patterns, colors, and yarns work together.

Strip combinations—For an interesting design that's also easy, make a fabric with diagonal stripes by alternating strips of different colors (or textures). Create another simple but beautiful fabric by alternating a plain stockinette-stitch strip with a reverse stockinette-stitch strip in the same color, which results in a diagonal ribbed effect, with seams either hidden or showing.

For multicolored strips, knitting blocks of color with the same number of rows gives an even checked or plaid pattern, as in Miyake's sweater, while irregular-length blocks create an uneven mixture. When sewing strips together, you can match the blocks to complete the smooth plaid effect, or stagger the color changes for a less regular stair-step effect.

Seaming—In sewing the strips together, you may decide to include another element of texture by placing the seams on the right side of the fabric, as Miyake did. Or for a smoother finish, sew the seams to the inside as usual. Either way, I use mattress stitch (see *Threads* No. 52, p. 20) to assemble the strips. Sewing is easier if I work 2 sts at each side of the strip in stockinette stitch, which gives a smooth edge for seaming.

Using diagonal strips in garments

While knitting, testing, and arranging my swatches, many ideas for applying the techniques to garments occurred to me, two of which I've sketched on p. 22 and above. Since sewing strips together is more time-consuming than some kinds of knitting, you might decide to try the technique in only a section of a garment, or use it to make hats and unusual scarves. I plan to use strips of knitting for a unique collar and some fancy slanted pockets to decorate a plain coat. And now that I've gotten a clear sense of how Miyake constructed his sweater, I am definitely planning a Miyake-inspired design for the future. □

Deborah Newton, author of Designing Knitwear *(The Taunton Press, 1992), wrote about designing with vertically placed strips in* Threads No. 45, pp. 51-55).

Design Knitwear from Sewing Patterns

The best part is there's no need to calculate tricky curves or slopes

by June Hemmons Hiatt

Don't be limited by the knitting patterns available. *You can design your own garment by starting with a sewing pattern, such as this vest designed by Issey Miyake. Although Vogue 1693 has been discontinued, a similar style, the Hong Kong Vest, is available from The Sewing Workshop (2010 Balboa St., San Francisco, CA 94121; 800-875-8824).*

have you wanted to design your own knits but weren't sure how to do it? Using sewing patterns as a starting point for knitting opens a rich new source of designs and also ensures a well-balanced garment and good fit.

There are two aspects of design that present challenges for many knitters. First, getting garment proportions and size correct can be difficult—the neckline may turn out too big, armholes too small, or sleeves too long. My approach provides a simple, accurate way to take measurements from a sewing pattern and translate them into a charted knitting pattern. You are, in effect, borrowing a garment shape created by a professional designer; what you add are the details of yarn type, color, and surface texture.

Second, many knitters fear the math calculations normally required to work out the pattern for a slope or curve. Most people, even professionals, avoid these problems by limiting their designs to very simple shapes. This method requires only the simplest calculator-assisted math. There's no need for complicated formulas to work out the pattern for slopes and curves—the instructions for these areas will simply appear on the chart as you draw the lines in.

Which patterns work?

Most sewing-pattern companies offer a wide selection of styles that adapt easily to knitting. At first, look for simple patterns with a minimum of seams and shaping. Until you gain confidence, avoid patterns with darts or seams in the bodice pieces.

Once you get the idea of how to use this method, you'll be able to use even complex patterns or blend elements from several patterns into one unique design. You can combine an interesting neckline from one pattern, for instance, with an asymmetrical opening or sleeve from another.

Refine the fit and shape—To prepare your pattern, cut the pieces apart outside the sewing lines and press flat. Make any necessary fitting alterations to the pattern, including sewing a test garment to check the fit, if needed.

Next, study the pattern and consider if it can be simplified by straightening any subtle curves or slopes that are required for shaping a sewn garment but aren't needed for a more flexible knitted one. For example, the curved center-back seam on the vest (see p. 28) was straightened and eliminated so the back could be knitted in one piece.

Consider the edge finishes— Also think now about how you want to finish the edges. The turned-back hems and facings used in sewing are generally bulky in knitting and are usually replaced by borders in a stitch pattern that lies very flat instead. Although ribbing is the most common nonrolling border, you can use a pattern such as seed stitch or add a crocheted border if you don't want the edge to draw in. As you can see, the front band of my vest on the facing page is ribbed, but because I wanted the main pattern to go all the way to the edge at the bottom and armhole, I faced these areas with fine-gauge ribbon.

You can knit a garment with the stitch pattern of your choice. The vest's delicate fern pattern is from Barbara Walker's A Second Treasury of Knitting Patterns *(Charles Scribner's Sons, 1970). Called the ribbed leaf, it's formed by twisting stitches every second row.*

Mark the waist and any dots that indicate joining points; draw lines that mark the true horizontal and vertical, as shown in the drawing on p. 28. Extend the center-front and -back lines up past the shoulder line to provide a guide for measurements you will take later.

Wherever an edge has a border that will be worked separately, consider whether this will add width or length to the piece. If so, you must remove an equal amount from the pattern to compensate. For any border area that's knitted as one with the garment section, draw a line showing where one stitch pattern ends and another begins. At this

Trace the pattern

Once you're satisfied with the shape of the garment, you're ready to copy the pattern. Cover each pattern piece with tracing paper, pin or weight it down, and use a pencil to outline each area you'll knit as a separate piece, tracing along the stitching lines. You don't need seam allowances, since just one extra stitch at each seam is needed to join knitting.

point, remove the original pattern from underneath the tracing paper to avoid confusing yourself with any extra lines.

Measure the key dimensions

Next, draw true horizontal and vertical lines defining the width and depth of each shaped area such as at the shoulder, neckline, and armhole, as shown in the drawing

on p. 28, and measure them. An L-shaped ruler is helpful here. Don't concern yourself now with the slopes and curves; measure only true horizontals and verticals.

Mark all measurements on the pattern pieces. Check to make sure that the front and back match at the neck width and along all seamlines. Once you're sure the pattern is complete and accurate, mark all the lines that define the finished pattern in colored pencil or marker and cut out the pieces.

An accurate gauge swatch is essential—In order to translate the pattern you've developed into one that you can knit from, you'll have to decide on the yarn and stitch or color pattern and make an accurate stitch gauge (see *Threads* No. 51, pp. 59-61). The gauge is the basis of knitting to size, so it's essential that it be accurate.

Turn measurements into stitches—Using a calculator and your stitch and row gauge, multiply all horizontal measurements by the stitch gauge and all vertical measurements by the row gauge. As you do the calculations, round the result up or down to whole numbers—you will, after all, be working with whole stitches. Write the required stitches and rows on

Most sewing-pattern companies offer a wide selection of styles that adapt easily to knitting.

the pattern adjacent to the measurement lines. Check the figures for accuracy; it helps to write down not just how many stitches must be added or subtracted but also how many will be on the needle before and after any increase or decrease.

Graph it!

Next, you'll make a chart by transferring the number of stitches and rows required onto regular graph paper with 10 squares/in. Each square of the graph paper represents one knitted stitch. There's no reason to chart an area unless it's shaped. For instance, if you're making a regular straight-sided garment, just write on your pattern how many stitches are required and how many rows to

knit from the lower edge to the armhole, then chart only the shaped areas of the armhole, shoulder, and neck, as shown in the top drawing on the facing page. Similarly, you don't have to chart both the front and back if they're the same in every respect but the neckline, nor do you need to chart more than half a front or back if both sides are symmetrical.

Working in pencil, draw a vertical line on your graph paper to define the center back. Starting with the back neck, as shown on the facing page, define the width and length of each shaped area by counting over the number of stitches and rows required, allowing one square per stitch and row.

Since real knit stitches are

rectangular, not square, the chart will *look* longer and narrower than the garment will actually knit up. Don't worry about the chart's shape—it will be an accurate guide to what you should do as you knit. I don't recommend knitters' graph paper; it's drawn in the proportion of five stitches and seven rows per inch and will only be accurate if your gauge is *exactly* that.

If you need a larger sheet of graph paper, you can tape pieces together or buy 11-by 14-in. graph paper (available at art-supply stores). Or break the pattern apart into component pieces, putting, for instance, the slope from wrist to underarm in one place on the graph paper and the curve for the sleeve cap in another.

Hocus-pocus—slopes and curves appear

After marking the widths and lengths of the shaped areas, draw in the slopes and curves. For the armhole, draw a smooth curve from the shoulder point to the underarm through the point that defines the narrowest width of the upper bodice. Then step off the stitches along the curve, following the lines of the graph paper, as in the top drawing on the facing page. This is the exciting part: The graph paper *shows* you the pattern to be knit—for example, when to decrease one stitch per row, one every other row, or one every fifth row. Next, draw in and step off the stitches for the neckline curve.

Draw a sloped line connect-

ADAPT A SEWING PATTERN FOR KNITTING

Let's look at the back of my vest pattern to learn how to prepare a sewing pattern for knitting. Although this pattern shape is a bit unusual, similar principles apply to any sewing pattern you choose.

Knitting gauge
9.25 st =1 in.
10 r = 1 in.

Step 1

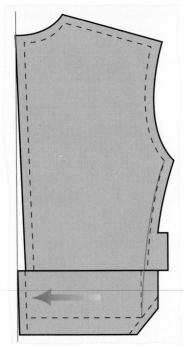

Steps 2-4

Horizontal from base of neck to first vertical line, then vertical up to end— for neck width and depth:
3.75 in. = 35 st
.875 in. = 8 r

Horizontal from shoulder at armhole to first vertical line, then vertical up to end—for shoulder width and depth:
6.5 in. = 60 st
1.5 in. = 16 r
(Needs to be even number of rows, so round up or down.)

Vertical for length from shoulder to hem
23.75 in. = 240 r

Horizontal from narrowest point of bodice to center:
10 in. x 2 = 185 st

Horizontal from base of armhole to center, then vertical at armhole up through deepest curve of armhole, to end—for armhole width and depth:
11 in. x 2 in. = 205 st
9.5 in. = 95 r

Original pattern

1. *Straighten center back so you can eliminate seam and knit back in one piece. Slice and shift bottom portion of pattern to prevent back from becoming too wide; redraw side seamline.*

Trace and measure pattern to knit

2. *Trace adjusted outline, removing facings and seam allowances. Draw horizontal and vertical lines that define shaped areas.*

3. *Measure all horizontal and vertical lines and note on pattern. If you've traced half the pattern, multiply measurement by two for full back or front width.*

4. *Translate inches to stitches: Multiply widths by stitch gauge, lengths by row gauge.*

ing the neckline to the armhole to define the shoulder slope. Since you'll be either casting off or, preferably, to get a smoother line, using short rows at the shoulder, you'll need to allow two rows for every group of stitches, as shown.

If your pattern has a sleeve, chart it in exactly the same way. That is, you'll translate horizontal and vertical measurements taken from the sewing pattern into stitches and rows on the graph paper, draw in the curve, and step off the pattern for the sleeve cap, as shown in the lower drawing at right.

Head off mistakes with guideposts

It helps to note row and stitch numbers at critical points of the pattern as shown, so you won't have to recount squares as you work. Check by adding up these numbers and dividing by the stitch or row gauge to ensure that all the widths and lengths are accurate before you begin knitting. Discover any mistakes now so you don't have to rip out your knitting later!

If you like, you can add additional notes to guide you as you knit. I write down the details of the yarn I'm using (manufacturer, color, yardage), the needle size and gauge, and the name and source of the stitch or color pattern (I attach a charted stitch or color pattern drawn on five- by five-square graph paper, if I need it).

If I'm knitting an intricate stitch or color pattern, I also like to draw in horizontal and vertical lines defining the stitch or color repeat so I know exactly how the surface pattern relates to the shaping for the armhole, neck, or shoulder. This helps me keep track of where I am while I'm knitting without the need to count rows. I often make a pencil mark showing where I am on the pattern when I put my work down, or I mark the pattern with a dot, row by row, as I knit curves or

slopes to keep my place.

The wonderful thing about this system is that it automatically provides you with the knitting pattern for all slopes and curves. You are, in effect, knitting on paper before you begin to knit in yarn—and it's much easier to erase and correct pencil mistakes than to rip and correct knitted ones. Once you get the hang of creating patterns with this method, you'll be able to knit any shape you want, refining your garments for greater comfort and style. Moreover, an accurate pattern means that you can relax and knit without worrying about whether your garment will turn out okay. □

June Hemmons Hiatt's book, The Principles of Knitting *(Simon and Schuster, 1988), functions as an essential guide for many knitters.*

YOU ONLY NEED TO CHART SHAPED SECTIONS

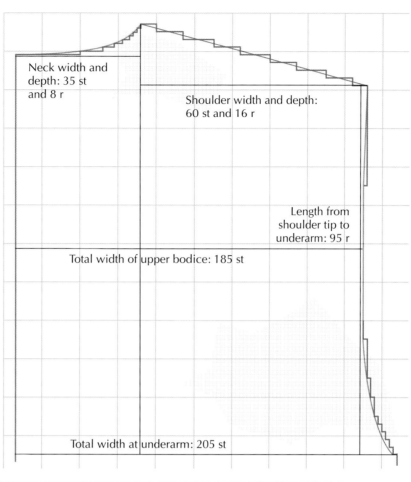

Neck width and depth: 35 st and 8 r

Shoulder width and depth: 60 st and 16 r

Length from shoulder tip to underarm: 95 r

Total width of upper bodice: 185 st

Total width at underarm: 205 st

Transfer curves and slopes to graph paper by drawing lines that define each shape; one square equals one stitch or row. Draw in each curve with pencil, then step off along squares. The shapes will look tall and narrow, but will knit up correctly.

While only upper quadrant is usually charted, note garment length from armhole and full garment length to check accuracy of other figures.

If Your Pattern Includes a Set-In Sleeve

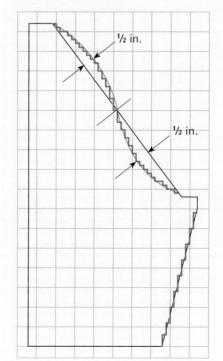

½ in.

½ in.

If, unlike a vest, your garment includes a sleeve, it's charted in exact same way. To make smooth S-curve for sleeve cap, first draw sloped line from sleeve cap to underarm as shown. Divide line into quarters, place dot ½ in. out from first mark and ½ in. in from third, and connect dots through center mark in smooth curve. Step off knitting pattern.

The slope from wrist to underarm is drawn and stepped off in normal way.

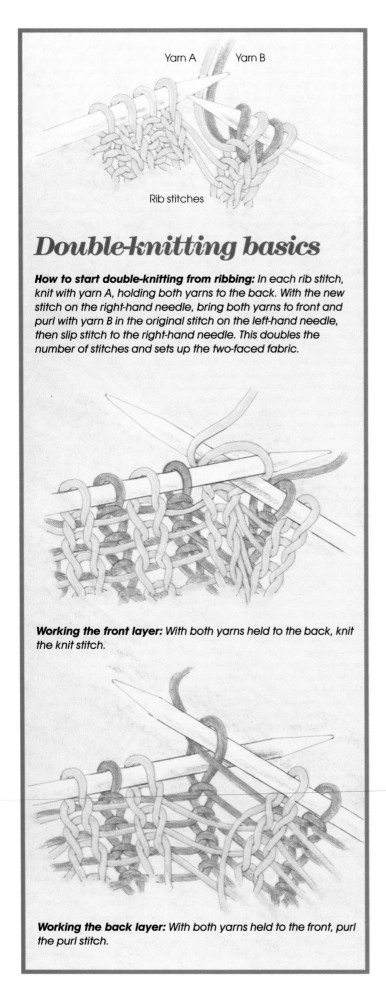

Yarn A **Yarn B**

Rib stitches

Double-knitting basics

How to start double-knitting from ribbing: In each rib stitch, knit with yarn A, holding both yarns to the back. With the new stitch on the right-hand needle, bring both yarns to front and purl with yarn B in the original stitch on the left-hand needle, then slip stitch to the right-hand needle. This doubles the number of stitches and sets up the two-faced fabric.

Working the front layer: With both yarns held to the back, knit the knit stitch.

Working the back layer: With both yarns held to the front, purl the purl stitch.

Reversible Knitting

Double knitting creates two layers of stockinette with one pass of stitches

by M'Lou Linsert Baber

about 10 years ago, I came across a knitted afghan pattern in a craft magazine, that used a stitch I hadn't seen before: a double stitch that made the afghan reversible. Intrigued, I tried a swatch. The technique was fun and fast, and I was hooked.

The trick of the double stitch is that you're working two layers of fabric, each in two colors, in every row. That is, while you're knitting jade green flowers on a black background, you're also knitting black flowers on jade green on the reverse side.

Although I loved double-knitting afghans, I wanted to use the technique for garments. The double stitch creates a fabric with two sides with air pockets between them. This insulation makes for a warm and cuddly knit

which I thought would be perfect for outerwear, such as sweaters, jackets, and hats. However, I couldn't find garment directions anywhere. I even wrote to the magazine asking for help. Nothing.

Undaunted, I decided to start small—with a baby sweater—and work out my own method of making reversible knitted garments. The swatch shown on p. 31 is an example of double knitting. Following is what I found.

Yarns

Finding the right yarn is extremely important because this double stitch is too heavy for garments in some yarns. For instance, worsted-weight yarn makes wonderful double-knit afghans but it's too bulky for garments. You'll have the best results with a finer yarn and smaller needles. However, even when you

Swatching with double knitting

Here's a practice pattern—little two-stitch by three-row squares dotted across a solid background—that would be a good swatch project. Or keep going and make a scarf.

If you're making a swatch, it should be at least 4 by 4 in. For a scarf, a good width is 8 in., unless you have a favorite scarf you can measure the width of. Cast on the number of stitches that equals the width of the swatch (or scarf) multiplied by the stitch gauge multiplied by two. Remember that half of the stitches will end up on the front (A) and the other half on the back (B). In sport-weight yarn that knits to a gauge of 5 sts/in. in double knitting, you'd cast on with color A 40 sts for a swatch and 80 sts for a scarf.

Row 1: Tie color B onto color A. *With both strands at back of work, knit 1 (k1) in color A. Bring both strands to front of work and purl 1 (p1) in color B. Repeat from * across. Half the stitches on your needle will be in color A, the other half in color B, and they will alternate across the row. At the end of the row, twist the yarns together to make a closed and firm edge.

Row 2: With both strands at the back of the work, k1 with color B. Bring both strands to front of work and p1 with color A. Repeat across the row. Twist the strands together.

Repeat rows 1 and 2 five times more, then repeat row 1. The pattern begins on row 14.

How to follow a chart in double knitting

Each square on the chart represents 2 sts—the knit stitch that faces you and the purl one on the reverse side. You always work the knit stitch first, and then you work the purl stitch in the contrast color.

On the odd-numbered rows, which you work from right to left, A is the background color. On even-numbered rows, which you work from left to right, B is the background color. Of course, if you're knitting on circular needles, you'll always be working the chart from right to left with A as the background color.

Knit the pattern stitches, marked with an X on the chart, in color B on the A side. Then purl the next stitch in color A. On the B side, do the opposite.

As an example, here's the first pattern row of the chart written out. Because this is an even-number row, B is the background color and the chart is worked from left to right.

Row 14: *(With both yarns in back, k1 with B, bring both yarns to front and p1 with A) four times; **(with both yarns in back, k1 with A, bring both yarns to front, and p1 with B) twice; (with both yarns in back, k1 with B, bring both yarns to front, and p1 with A) eight times. Repeat from ** across row, ending last repeat from * to **. Twist yarns.

To finish the swatch, simply tie off color B and, using color A, knit both the A and B stitches as one across the row. On the next row, bind off. To finish the scarf, make a fringed edge. —*M.B.*

A scarf with a simple pattern is a good introduction to reversible knitting. Each square on the chart represents two stitches (one in front, one in back) on the needle.

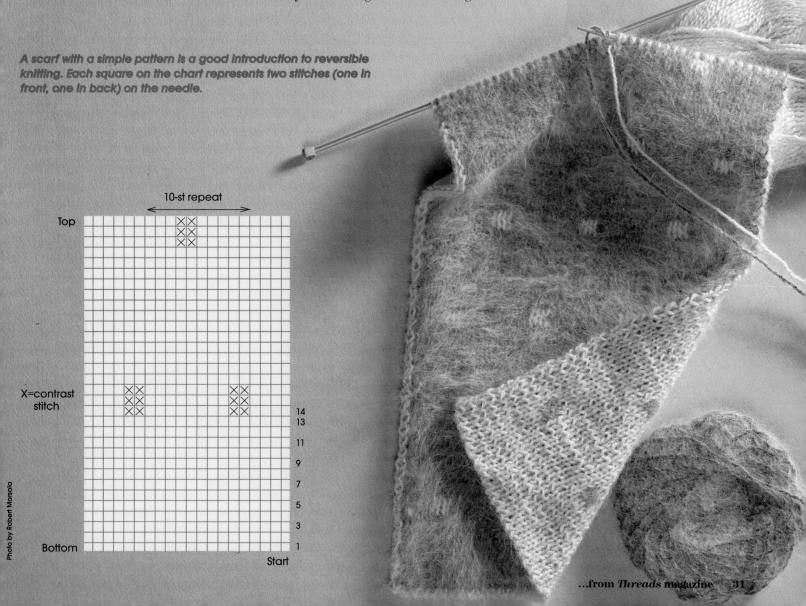

Photo by Robert Marsala

10-st repeat

Top

X=contrast stitch

Bottom

Start

14
13
11
9
7
5
3
1

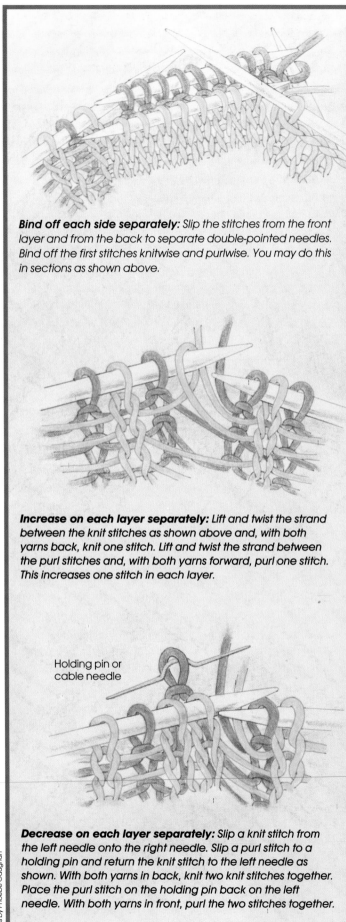

Bind off each side separately: *Slip the stitches from the front layer and from the back to separate double-pointed needles. Bind off the first stitches knitwise and purlwise. You may do this in sections as shown above.*

Increase on each layer separately: *Lift and twist the strand between the knit stitches as shown above and, with both yarns back, knit one stitch. Lift and twist the strand between the purl stitches and, with both yarns forward, purl one stitch. This increases one stitch in each layer.*

Holding pin or cable needle

Decrease on each layer separately: *Slip a knit stitch from the left needle onto the right needle. Slip a purl stitch to a holding pin and return the knit stitch to the left needle as shown. With both yarns in back, knit two knit stitches together. Place the purl stitch on the holding pin back on the left needle. With both yarns in front, purl the two stitches together.*

use smaller needles, this stitch tends to spread. For example, if you want to make a pattern that calls for a worsted-weight gauge of 5 sts/in., you'll achieve that gauge with sport-weight yarn (which normally knits at about 6 sts/in. And if you want to get 6 sts/in. in a reversible garment, you'll need to go to a fingering- or baby-weight yarn.

Yarns that are tightly twisted also add undesirable weight to garments. The best bets are soft, lightweight yarns with a loose twist. A fluffy yarn with mohair works well too. I've had good results with washable acrylic/wool blends for children's sweaters and hats.

Patterns

You can adapt patterns you already have to double knitting. However, as mentioned before, the double-stitch gauge will be completely different from the recommended gauge for that yarn. So here are my guidelines for swatching: Start with two colors in a yarn you love. Experimenting with needle sizes, make swatches until you get a fabric you like. (See "Swatching with double knitting" on p. 31 for specifics on how to swatch in double knitting.) Measure the gauge of your swatch, *only counting the stitches on one side*. Then find a pattern to match the stitch-per-inch gauge you've achieved. The double stitch works up more squat than most other stitches, so your row count probably won't match the pattern's at all. But that's okay, because you can work additional rows until you get the length, in inches, that you need. However, make sure that the double stitches don't distort two-color patterns, such as Fair Isle, by squashing the design too much.

To avoid sewing side seams, I try to find patterns in which the fronts and back are knit in one piece to the underarm. (I'll explain how to handle the seams at shoulders, necklines, and armholes.)

I also like to look for a pattern that has ribbing at the bottom and cuffs. You rib in one color, and to begin the body of your double-knit garment, you simply make an extra stitch in each ribbing stitch with the contrast color (see the top drawing on p. 30).

Special techniques

If you decide to make a cardigan, you can finish the front edges with ribbing, knitting it in vertically as you go. All you have to remember is to twist the yarns together right before you change to a single color for the ribbing, and again when you change from a single yarn back to two yarns for the double knitting. You can also use other flat, noncurling stitches, such as garter and seed stitch, for cardigan borders. I make the buttonholes in one front band and put buttons on both sides of the other band.

In a cardigan that's knit in one piece to the underarms, I like to work the fronts and backs separately to the shoulders. As I work from the underarms to the shoulders, I don't twist the yarns at the armhole edges. This gives you two separate layers at the armholes. After you finish the fronts and back and sew the shoulder seams, you knit the sleeves from the armhole down. With a circular needle and the matching background color, you pick up stitches around the armhole on one side. Then with another circular needle and the contrasting color, you pick up the stitches on the other side. With a third circular needle, on the next row, you blend the colors as you would for double knitting, by knitting and purling according to your chart, from alternate needles onto the third needle.

Bind off each shoulder seam separately, as shown in the top drawing at left. Then, using yarn that matches the background color, sew the seam from the right side. Turn the work over and sew the other side. One of the beauties of double knitting is that, after finishing, all yarn ends can be pulled between the two layers of the garment where they won't show.

It's also important to keep the two sides separate when increasing and decreasing stitches. See the two lower drawings on the facing page.

When you're going from double knit to neckband ribbing in a single color, you need to decrease half the stitches in the double-knit section. Knit the double stitches together, with the knit stitch facing you and its contrasting purl stitch, across the row. If you need to pick up stitches from shaped areas of the front neckline, treat both layers as one. Knit twice the neckband width, fold it over, and sew it down neatly on the other side. This makes a nice reversible band.

Buttonholes can be made in the double-knit fabric by following the technique used for binding off. The difference is that you'll put on the double-pointed needles the number of stitches for the buttonhole, plus the one extra that's left over when the buttonhole bind-off is complete. Or, if you prefer, instead of using double-pointed needles, you can slip the stitches onto a cable holder. After you finish knitting your garment, a final step is to sew the buttonhole edges together.

If this technique for double knitting seems difficult to understand, try it anyway. I'm sure that you'll be as delighted and amazed as I was.   □

M'Lou Linsert Baber is an artist and knitter who lives in Nampa, ID. She is presently at work on a book of double-knit garments.

A technique used to make reversible knitted blankets inspired a series of garments, including this "Mille-fleurs" sweater. Most Fair Isle two-color patterns can be adapted to double knitting, in which both sides of the fabric are knit at the same time.

Knitting a Basketweave Look-Alike

Here's how to work and shape entrelac on a circular needle

by Gwen Fox

entrelac is an unusual knitting pattern that produces fabric that looks like basket-woven strips of stockinette. This beautiful stitch is composed of alternating rows of opposing rectangles, which are worked one rectangle at a time and which hang diagonally from one corner (see the photo on the facing page). Most patterns instruct knitters to work the garment front and back separately in large, squarish pieces and sew them together for a typically boxy, dropped-shoulder sweater. But the awkward bulk resulting from unshaped sleeves and shoulders and from the added presence of side seams diminishes the potential beauty of an entrelac garment.

At about the time I discovered this stitch, I was knitting seamless yokes in the round for modified sweatshirts. Since I'm an avid seamless knitter, I began to wonder if it was possible to knit entrelac on a circular needle and avoid seams. And I also began trying to figure out how to shape entrelac fabric without distorting its basic rectangular units.

With only a little experimentation, I realized I could, indeed, knit entrelac in the round. I would still have to work the

Traditionally knitted flat, the entrelac pattern can instead be worked in the round to eliminate seams and be shaped with graduated rectangles to reduce bulk in the shoulders, neck, and sleeves.

Knitting entrelac in the round

Entrelac is a four-step pattern composed of alternating rounds of opposing rectangles, bordered top and bottom by a round of triangles. The fabric is created one triangle or rectangle at a time by working only a portion of stitches held on a circular needle. The rectangles always have twice as many rows as stitches.

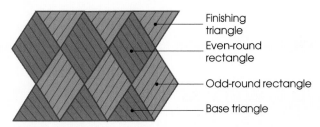

- Finishing triangle
- Even-round rectangle
- Odd-round rectangle
- Base triangle

Knitting abbreviations	
dec	decrease
k	knit
ndl	needle
no	number
p	purl
rep	repeat
rem	remaining
RS	right side
sl	slip
st(s)	stitch(es)
ssk	slip, slip, knit
tog	together
WS	wrong side

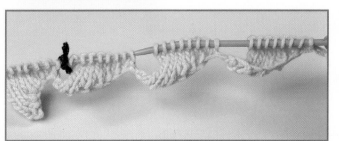

Completed base triangles (seen here from RS, with marker after first triangle) look rather odd on the needle before the first round of rectangles is worked.

1 Knitting base triangles: On circular ndl, cast on (or pick up) total no. of sts. *With RS facing, k2. Turn work and p WS. K3 on RS, adding next st on ndl. P WS. Continue to k additional st on RS and p WS up to last st to be k on RS. K st, * sl marker onto ndl to note completion of first triangle. Rep from * to * to make other triangles. ⇨

From *Threads* magazine (June 1994) 53:62-66

individual rectangles one at a time, knitting the right side and purling the wrong side, but the garment as a whole could be worked in the round. In fact, I found it was easier to work an entrelac cylinder on a circular needle than to work it flat and seam the edges. And besides, the fabric was far handsomer without seams.

Next I tackled how to shape the fabric. Since entrelac's integrity relies on maintaining the basic units' rectangular shape, any increase or decrease of stitches to shape the fabric had to leave the basic rectangle unaltered. After experimenting a bit, the answer suddenly dawned on me: rows of rectangles that graduated in size.

When I made the sweater shown on p. 34, I began by knitting each sleeve in the round up to the base of the armhole. Then I knitted the sweater body in the round up to the same point, slipped the sleeve stitches onto the same needle as the body, and joined them by knitting up the sweater's yoke. The only seam in the sweater is a short one under each arm.

I chose two differently textured yarns in the same color to subtly show off the patterning: a sport-weight angora and flat rayon tape. Using different colors of yarn for the alternating rows would likewise highlight the pattern.

Planning an entrelac sweater

Because the entrelac rectangles hang on the bias, the fabric tends to stretch. The degree of stretch depends on the weight and elasticity of the yarn you choose. Very elastic yarns like wools work far better for entrelac projects than inelastic yarns like cottons.

Because of this stretch and the pattern's visual complexity, a simple, loose-fitting pullover is a good style for a first project. To keep matters uncomplicated and the garment seamless, the pullover should have a yoke rather than raglan sleeves. Once you've mastered the process of making a yoked entrelac sweater, you can try a garment with more unusual shaping and details.

Getting a length gauge—Given the pattern's tendency to stretch, think of gauge as a ballpark estimate. After deciding on the general measurements for your sweater (body and sleeve length and hip and chest width), borrowing those from a favorite loose-fitting pullover if you want, use the following method to determine your ballpark length gauge.

Knit a flat stockinette swatch in your yarn that's 25 stitches wide by 50 rows long (entrelac always has twice as many rows as stitches). Because of the pattern's stretch, it's not crucial to block the swatch before taking your gauge. Then use straight pins to mark a rectangle the size you want in the center of the swatch, being sure it has twice as many rows as stitches. Next measure the rectangle's diagonal length, which tells you what the vertical length will be of one row—or, to be more precise, round, since you'll be working on a circular needle— of entrelac rectangles. (Although the pattern unit is based on two rounds of rectangles, the

2 **Knitting first (odd-numbered) round of rectangles:** With WS facing, pick up sts for rectangle on left edge of triangle, working from top to base (a crochet hook may help pick up sts). Turn and k RS. *On WS, p to last st and p this st tog with first st of base triangle to left to join sections. (See Threads No. 53, p. 20.) K RS. * Rep from * to * to incorporate all sts on triangle. Rep process on each triangle.

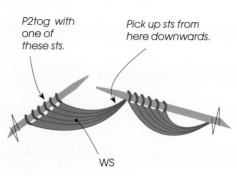

P2tog with one of these sts.

Pick up sts from here downwards.

WS

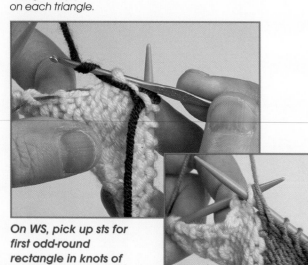

On WS, pick up sts for first odd-round rectangle in knots of sts on selvage edge.

Purl together sts to join sections at the end of a purl row.

3 **Knitting second (even-numbered) round of rectangles:** With RS facing, pick up and k req no. of sts on left (top) selvage edge of odd-round rectangle, working from top to base of V. P WS. *On RS, k to last st. Sl st as if to k, sl first st of last rectangle to left as if to k; reinsert left ndl in front of these sts and ktog (ssk) to join sections. P WS. * Rep from * to * to incorporate all sts on first rectangle. Rep process on each rectangle.

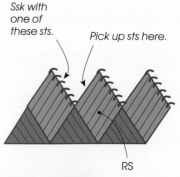

Ssk with one of these sts.

Pick up sts here.

RS

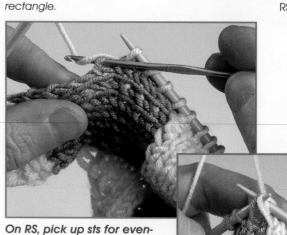

On RS, pick up sts for even-round rectangles in end sts on selvage edge.

Use an ssk to join sections at the end of a knit row.

even-numbered rounds only fill in the fabric but don't add length to it.)

Start your length calculations by marking and measuring the largest rectangle you'd like to use in the body of your sweater (try drawing entrelac "fabric" on a piece of paper and holding it up to you to see if the rectangles look too large or small for the sweater body). Then pin-mark your swatch anew and measure, one by one, the increasingly smaller rectangles you need to shape the garment. By dividing the diagonal length of each size rectangle into the length needed for a given part of your garment, you can figure out how many rounds of rectangles you need to knit.

For example, when I swatched and measured the diagonal length of the large rectangle for the bottom part of my sweater, it measured 4 in. So I needed four odd-numbered rounds of rectangles to produce the 16 in. I wanted from the base triangles (which, like the even-numbered rounds of rectangles, fill the fabric but

don't add length) to the underarm. (If your calculations produce a fraction, round up to the nearest whole number.)

Getting a stitch gauge—To figure out the number of stitches needed for the sweater's bottom edge, first divide the sweater's hip measurement by the diagonal length of your largest rectangle. This tells you how many rectangles you need to knit in the round. (Dividing the 4-in. diagonal length of my largest rectangle into the 48-in. hip measurement I wanted for my sweater, I found I needed to work 12 rectangles.) Then count the number of stitches in your largest rectangle and multiply that by the number of rectangles you need to knit. (My rectangle had 12 stitches, so I had to cast on 144 stitches for the 12 rectangles I needed.)

Ribbing for entrelac—Unlike working ribbing on most sweaters, you don't need to decrease the number of stitches for ribbing on an entrelac sweater. The pattern

stitch will naturally make the fabric wider than the ribbing, and decreasing stitches for ribbing would create an unattractively blousy effect. You don't even need to use a smaller needle than the one you used for the body to keep the ribbing from stretching.

Planning the yoke

After planning the bottom part of the sweater, figure out the yoke, working from the neck down (you'll be knitting the yoke from the bottom up, but it's easier to plan from the neck down). While you can use any size rectangle in the lower part of the sweater, I suggest planning the triangles and rectangles at the neck to be five or four stitches wide, and never less than four. Four or five stitches are easy to work with, and the scale of pattern they produce is flattering near the face.

To simplify calculations, plan the yoke to be either five or seven rounds deep, counting both odd- and even-numbered rounds of rectangles in addition to the

---

4 ***Knitting finishing triangles:*** After an even round of rectangles *(see drawing at right)—Pick up required no. of sts as for odd-round rectangles. K RS. *On WS, p up to last st and ptog with first st of base rectangle to right. K all but last st on RS. P WS, as above. On RS, k1 fewer end sts than on last round. * Rep from * to * to incorporate all sts on first rectangle.*

If you need to dec for shaping (as for a yoke), p3tog, with 2 sts from rectangle for each dec needed, halfway through making triangle.

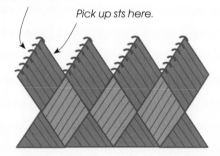

After even round of rectangles, p2tog with one of these sts.

Pick up sts here.

*After an odd round of rectangles (see photo below)—Pick up required no. of sts as for even-round rectangles. P WS. *On RS, k up to last st. Ssk this st tog with first st of base rectangle to left. P all but last st on WS. K RS as above. On WS, p 1 fewer end sts than on last round. * Rep from * to * to incorporate all sts on first rectangle.*

If you need to dec for shaping (as for a yoke), work ssk with 2 sts from rectangle (3 sts altog) for each dec needed, halfway through making triangle. Rep process around edge, leaving rem sts to be cast off or k into ribbing or another part of garment.

You can cast off, rib, or knit another part of garment with sts of finishing triangles (worked here after an odd round of rectangles).

Planning and knitting an entrelac sweater

The drawings below show the measurements and stitch counts worked out for the entrelac pullover on p. 34.

1. Knit sleeves on circular needles.

2. Knit body on circular needle.

3. Move sleeves to circular needle with body, and join by knitting yoke.

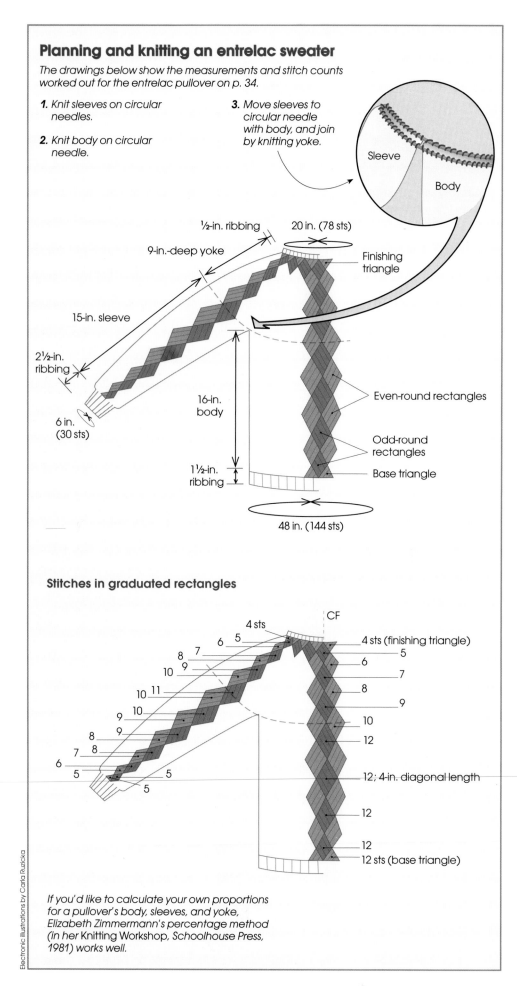

Sleeve

Body

½-in. ribbing

20 in. (78 sts)

9-in.-deep yoke

Finishing triangle

15-in. sleeve

2½-in. ribbing

Even-round rectangles

16-in. body

Odd-round rectangles

6 in. (30 sts)

1½-in. ribbing

Base triangle

48 in. (144 sts)

Stitches in graduated rectangles

CF

4 sts

4 sts (finishing triangle)

5   5
6   6
8 7   7
10 9   8
10 11   9
10 10   10
9   12
9 8
7 8   12; 4-in. diagonal length
6
5 5   12
5
                12

                12

                12 sts (base triangle)

If you'd like to calculate your own proportions for a pullover's body, sleeves, and yoke, Elizabeth Zimmermann's percentage method (in her Knitting Workshop, *Schoolhouse Press, 1981) works well.*

finishing round of triangles. The smoothest shaping is produced with gradual decreases on each round of rectangles, not just the odd-numbered rounds. From the neck down, the rectangles in each round will become one stitch wider. In my sweater, the yoke was seven rounds deep, including the finishing triangle, which was four stitches wide at the top (see the schematic at left).

As with calculating length on the bottom part of the sweater, figure out the yoke depth by adding up the diagonal length of the rectangles in each odd-numbered round, starting with the round just before the finishing round of triangles and ending with the round at the base of the underarm. (In my sweater, these odd-round rectangles measured 2½, 2¾, and 3¾ in., making my yoke a total of 9 in. deep.)

Tips for knitting entrelac

In the process of working on several entrelac projects, I discovered a few techniques that improve the look of the knitting. The most important one is picking up stitches for new rectangles in the knots, or end stitches, on the selvage edge (see the photo at left on p. 36). This is the firmest part of the fabric and prevents the holes that would form if you knitted or purled between rows. Working into these end stitches also helps space the stitches evenly along the edge. You may find it helpful to use a crochet hook to pick up the stitches.

Another useful technique for working entrelac is knitting backwards (see *Threads* No. 53, p. 20). Since each rectangle needs to be knitted flat despite working the whole garment in the round, you'll find it far less tedious and time-consuming to knit backwards rather than turning the work every few stitches to knit or purl the next row.

Finally, note that you can work entrelac in the round by casting on, using live stitches, or picking up stitches. Similarly, you can cast off the last row of the finishing triangles or leave them live and knit ribbing or another part of the sweater. This means that entrelac can be worked for an entire pullover or just for a yoke, sleeves, band at the sweater's bottom edge, or even cuffs. Once you've mastered the basic technique, I hope you'll find designing with entrelac as much fun as I do. □

Gwen Fox is a computer programmer and avid knitter in Fresno, CA. The complete pattern for her sweater is available from her for $5 postpaid at 1025 E. Griffith Way, Fresno, CA 93704.

A Balancing Act

Knitter's guide to pattern and proportion

by Alice Korach

When I began designing Fair Isle sweaters, my best looking garments invariably turned out to have two main pattern bands, in relative sizes of approximately 5 to 8. So I kept doing minor variations, wondering why this proportion yields such consistently satisfying sweaters. Eventually I researched the mathematics as deeply as a high-school math-phobe could and found some intriguing facts to support what my eyes and intuition had already told me.

Fortunately, one doesn't have to be a math wizard to use these principles in sweater design. Adding, subtracting, multiplying, and dividing are all that are needed. It helps to have an inexpensive, pocket-sized calculator; a notebook; and a critical design eye.

First, let's look at the mathematical concepts on which these basic design principles are based. Then we'll see how to bend the rules to make Fair Isles and Arans that please us with their fit and their beauty.

The golden ratio

I wouldn't know what to do with a logarithm if I fell over one. But I do know one thing about logs: mathematicians devised them to describe natural measurements that, for whatever reason, are found so pervasively throughout the physical universe. For example, the beautiful chambered nautilus shell grows in a perfect logarithmic sequence; and roses space their buds at logarithmic intervals along a stem.

Artists and designers who seek to reproduce the beauty and harmony of nature have long recognized the consistent recurrence of this special ratio, in which the proportion of the whole to a part equals the proportion of that part to the remainder. The ratio is, very nearly, 8 to 5 or about 62%. Pythagoras, the Greek mathematician who loved the mystery and unity to be found in numbers (and developed much of the geometry taught in high school today), was especially intrigued by this ratio,

which he called the "golden ratio." Kepler called it the "divine proportion." The sides of a golden rectangle, formed from a square and an arc, as shown, form this ratio. You can see it in nearly any kind of human design from the elegant Greek Parthenon to Le-Corbusier's buildings. And when we design a piece of fiberwork today, it looks more natural to us when we incorporate the golden ratio.

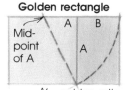

Golden rectangle

Mid-point of A

A/B = golden ratio

A slight extension of the golden ratio for which we will have plenty of use in Aran designs is the Fibonacci series. It's a list of numbers constructed as follows:

a) the first number in the series is 1;
b) the second number in the series is 1;
c) the third number is the sum of the previous two numbers;
d) and each successive number is also the sum of the previous two numbers.

The series, which begins 1, 1, 2, 3, 5, 8, 13, 21, 34, can go for as long as you want to add numbers. What is interesting about this series is that as it gets longer, the ratio of two successive numbers becomes increasingly closer to the true golden ratio.

Designing Fair Isle sweaters

Most traditional Fair Isle sweater patterns consist of two alternating sizes of horizontal pattern bands, each pair of bands being separated by a narrow border stripe. What raises the sweater from merely a good pattern to a work of art is how the rules are delicately bent.

A successful Fair Isle sweater is the result of a careful balance of the number of pattern bands, patterns within each band, contrast between bands, and the manner in which the many colors (but only two per round) are distributed in the total design. If any of these aspects becomes too complex, the sweater turns out random-looking; if any aspect is too simple, the sweater

ends up ungainly and ugly. Each band's unique pattern should stand out just enough to contrast with the other bands.

Fitting pattern bands to length—Most Fair Isle pattern bands are knitted on an odd number of rows, being composed of the same number of rows above and below a single, pivotal row. The odd numbers in most pattern heights allow you to find many usable combinations that approach the 62% golden ratio. By pairing up pattern bands whose relative proportion nearly matches the golden ratio, you can achieve a remarkably satifying result: 7- and 11-row patterns work well with 3-row dividers; similar ratios and effects occur with 9 and 15 rows, 11 and 17, 11 and 19, and 13 and 21.

Larger pattern repeats are only realistic for gigantic sweaters knitted for Paul Bunyans; for most of us, they don't allow enough pattern bands to make an appealing sweater. An adult's sweater (aprroximately 22 in. long from shoulder to rib top) on size 4 or 5 needles would allow approximately 120-130 pattern rows from rib to shoulder, or at least five bands each of 7- and 11-row patterns with 3-row dividers. I don't like to knit a sweater with fewer than 10 pattern bands—it makes the wearer look fat. A denser gauge with size 1 to 3 needles, requiring more rows, gives the designer greater flexibility in terms of pattern height and number of bands.

The two pattern bands, requiring an odd number of rows, are never even multiples of each other. This is fortunate, because the visual tension created by "almost but not quite" doubling of band heights keeps a design from looking repetitive and boring. This tension can be reinforced by making the small dividing pattern an even number of rows tall (usually 2 or 4 rows).

When you begin to plan a Fair Isle sweater (box, page 41), you must know your gauge exactly before you calculate the number of rows from rib-top to underarm and underarm to shoulder. Only then can you appor-

Arans and Fair Isles, or any designs built on re-peating patterns will be most satisfying when some simple rules of proportion are followed. If you want a unified pattern that works out neat-ly and completely, take the time to do some simple calculations. (Photo by John Kane)

tion pattern rows among the total rows and end up with a perfect-fitting sweater. You can, of course, gain a few more or a few less rows by decreasing or increasing needle size. The fun comes in making length and pat-tern heights come out evenly; a broken half-pattern at the top or bottom is not at all pro-fessional. There are an endless number of ways to make the design work out: begin-ning or ending with the dividing pattern; be-ginning or ending with the large pattern; be-ginning or ending with the small pattern; or using a single, exceptionally tall chest band. This also can create an interesting visual contrast, giving a clearer image of the kind of detail to be seen in each band or showcasing a particularly complex band pattern.

Fitting repeats around the body—A con-summate Fair Isle mathematician not only calculates total rows and pattern row height alternations so no broken patterns result, he or she also chooses or modifies patterns so that the chosen number of repeats exactly fit the number of stitches around the body. If this is not possible, which it sometimes isn't, the pattern break should occur under one or both armholes. Large, important-looking pat-terns should be centered front and back.

You have to experiment with all sorts of cal-culations and arrangements. There's no end to the possibilities, but there's no shortcut either. (For details on Fair Isle knitting tech-niques, see *Threads* No. 8, p. 44 and No. 20, p. 34, and the books by Sheila McGregor and Alice Starmore listed at the end of this article.)

Designing Aran sweaters

Aran sweaters, like most good designs, abide by the golden ratio. In a classical Aran design, the center vertical panel occupies between 36% and 40% of the front or back half, and the remaining 64% to 60% is divided between the cable panels, which may be of varied width, texture, and relief, arranged in a mirror image along either side of the central panel. The proportional division of the vertical cable panels will be especially pleasing if you appor-tion them in a Fibonacci-type progression.

Apportioning panels—Suppose, for exam-ple, your finished sweater is 40 in. around, so front and back are each 20 in. wide. A pleasing center panel will be about 7½ in. wide; there remain 6¼ in. on each side for laying out the vertical cables.

The first six members of the Fibonacci se-ries—1, 1, 2, 3, 5, and 8—add up to 20. But while a sweater designed with 1 in., 1 in., 2 in., 3 in., 5 in., and 8 in. patterns should be very appealing, the garment would be enor-mous if we want to repeat the narrow panels on each side of the central 8 in. panel.

Fortunately, the effect of the Fibonacci se-

A Nine-color Fair Isle

Begin with the basics—I love jumper weight Shetland two-ply. It gives me a *gauge* of 7 sts and 8 rows per in. on size 2 needles. Find your gauge by knitting at least a 6-in. swatch, stranded and in the round, then cutting and measuring.

Measure the chest, and, because stranded knitting always pulls in a little, be sure to add at least 4 in. ease for most sweaters. This one will be about 46 in. around. With arms at the sides, measure from the place on the hip where the wrist rests naturally. This will give sufficient *length* (approximately 21½ in.) to allow the sleeve patterns to match body patterns exactly if they start about 4 in. below the shoulder join.

Planning pattern widths—Multiply chest size by st gauge. You want a number that will divide into many different multiples. If it doesn't, add rather than subtract. I came up with 45½ x 7 = 318½, so I started by trying patterns that repeat evenly in 320 stitches: ten 32-st lozenge-with-cross combinations. You can also easily modify a standard pattern (from McGregor or elsewhere) to fit that multiple. Many lozenges have squared-off corners. You can simply extend the corner by one stitch on the center row to make a point.

For the smaller bands, select patterns where the number of stitches per pattern repeat divides perfectly into 320. Thus, patterns with repeats of 8, 10, and 16 work, but repeats of 9, 12, or 15 do not. These work fine above the armhole, however, where the patterns are broken anyway.

Planning the two pattern-band heights—Calculate the approximate number of pattern rows (length x row gauge) and see what large multiples fit. On my sweater, which is 21½ x 8 = 172 pattern rows tall, 15-row lozenge patterns work nicely with 9-row chain patterns and 5-row dividers (a repeat of a 5-9-5-15 or 34-row pattern). To see how many bands you'll have, divide the total number of rows (172) by the number of rows in the full repeat (34). It comes out almost perfectly (5 times, with 2 left over). Add a 5-row divider on top, giving 175 rows. (Actually, 174 rows, since the last solid-color row is used to graft the front and back together.) That is close enough.

The sweater will alternate 9- and 15-row bands five times (giving 10 bands total), with a five-row band between each pattern and at both the bottom and top. Of course, I choose a different pattern for each band. The five-row dividing band is a variation of the four-row tooth-like pattern (from McGregor), with a solid-color row on both the top and bottom. Its multiple is 4, which goes into 320 eighty times.

Calculating when to start the armhole—I always make a chart listing the number of rows in each pattern group. Then, if I want 100 rows before the armhole, I just add up rows, counting up from the bottom, and in this case I start the steek (armhole opening) on the eighth row of the last band of the third full repeat (the 100th row).

To highlight the chest band, I kept to a 15-row band, but instead of a lozenge, used an anchor motif that's a bit narrower. I set each anchor exactly above the cross on the lozenge band and choose a different, wider cross to set above the lozenge.

Sleeves begin with the divider pattern above the fourth full multiple (that is, slightly above midpoint on the armhole), so that they'll repeat the body, and end at the cuff on the same repeat as the waist rib does.

The neck is slightly shaped with a steek knitted into the front for the last 18 rows. The neck band keeps the same proportions of the 3-inch ribs but the number of rows are lessened by one for each color so the overall rib is only 2 inches high.

The corrugated rib has a 6-stitch multiple, and it doesn't stretch as much as an ordinary rib, so plan to increase only minimally, if at all, for the body.

Fair Isle Calculations: Apportioning pattern bands along sweater length

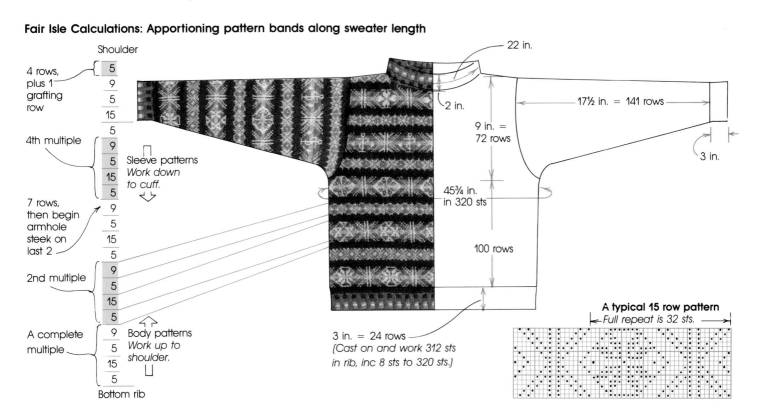

Shoulder

4 rows, plus 1 grafting row
5 / 9 / 5 / 15

4th multiple
5 / 9 / 5 / 15 / 5
Sleeve patterns *Work down to cuff.*

7 rows, then begin armhole steek on last 2
9 / 5 / 15 / 5

2nd multiple
9 / 5 / 15 / 5

A complete multiple
9 / 5 / 15 / 5
Body patterns *Work up to shoulder.*

Bottom rib

22 in.

2 in.

17½ in. = 141 rows

9 in. = 72 rows

45¾ in. in 320 sts

3 in.

100 rows

3 in. = 24 rows *(Cast on and work 312 sts in rib, inc 8 sts to 320 sts.)*

A typical 15 row pattern
Full repeat is 32 sts.

ries will not be lost if you fudge a little. You can even omit a number without losing the effect of the progression. When you come up with a series of intervals that nearly adds up to your total, you can choose and swatch your cable patterns. Then fine-tune your design, fleshing it out to the correct width. You may need to separate the panels with an additional twist knit stitch or two, decrease each element proportionally, or omit one cable per side. See the box at right for a detailed example. Twisted stitches (knit in back) provide an effective frame for the panels, but if their omission would yield the desired size, panels could be separated by alternating knit and purl backgrounds, which create a much subtler effect.

Cable gauges and multiples—Gauges of cable stitches vary depending on the relief and density of the pattern. Cables formed of twist stitches are only a bit tighter than a basic stockinette gauge in the same wool and needles, but those that cross two to four stitches become increasingly more dense. An Aran that alternates twist and cross patterns may require 30% more stitches than a stockinette sweater would. Obviously, when designing an Aran, you must knit swatches for every cable and measure carefully, choosing those panels that, when combined, produce the desired size. You must also swatch and calculate the number of stitches for the rib carefully since you'll require far fewer than you would expect, looking just at your total stitch count for the cabled patterns.

Because cables so commonly cross two stitches over two, four is frequently the basic multiple in cable patterns, with complicated braids being 8, 16, 32, 40, or more stitches wide. It is easy to find cable and twist patterns based on four stitch multiples. Though the gauges may vary, keeping to the same multiple can add subtle harmony to the overall appearance of a sweater. A canny Aran designer will think carefully about how to use cables with varying gauges to add some visual tension to a sweater design, much as she uses uneven size multiples in Fair Isle patterns.

The same goes for vertical repeats. If you choose cables that all repeat over the same number of rows, your sweater will look machine-made and dull. But narrow cables that repeat every four rows alternated with 8-row or 16-row repeat cables on slightly wider panels and 32- or 36-row repeats on a wide center panel yield a most harmonious result. Ideally, the central, widest panel would repeat at the largest multiple of four.

No one may notice that your prize Aran is built on the number four, but everyone will comment on how beautiful the sweater is. A mathematically designed Aran with panels that also follow the Fibonacci series conveys a subtle rightness that is obvious to all, even though few people could explain the reason.

Gauge adjustments

One of the very frustrating features of designing any sweater is that after you have selected patterns and planned their arrangement according to a particular design, the size of the garment turns out to be wrong. You should never lock yourself into a particular gauge. If only a minor adjustment is needed, you can increase needle size by one or two to get a larger garment or decrease needle size for a smaller one. Different yarns will also increase or decrease gauge.

In Fair Isle designs I prefer to go smaller and knit a finer gauge to get a more detailed pattern, if any adjustment is needed. With Arans the situation is different. Very tight cables are hard to turn, so you can't go too much smaller than the optimal gauge. On the other hand, you can't go much larger either, or the cables look loose and sloppy. It is preferable to make an Aran pattern bigger by adding a cable or a few moss or seed stitches on each side, if you need a lot of expansion. The only ways to make an Aran pattern significantly smaller are to delete panels or to start over on a new design. Plan slightly small and work up to the perfect size; it saves restarts.

Whatever you have to do to make your numerical plan work in a sweater is worth the effort, though. A carefully calculated garment reveals a unity and perfection that more than repays the math time. □

Alice Korach is an associate editor of Threads *Magazine.*

Further reading

Huntley, H.E., *The Divine Proportion: A study in Mathematical Beauty.* New York: Dover Publications, Inc., 1970.

McGregor, Sheila. *The Complete Book of Traditional Fair Isle Knitting.* New York: Charles Scribners Sons, 1981.

Starmore, Alice, *Alice Starmore's Book of Fair Isle Knitting.* Newtown, CT: The Taunton Press, 1989.

Thompson, Gladys, *Patterns for Guernseys, Jerseys and Arans.* New York: Dover Publications, Inc., 1979 (GT).

Walker, Barbara G. *Charted Knitting Designs, A Third Treasury of Knitting Patterns.* New York: Charles Scribners Sons, 1972 (BWIII); *A Second Treasury of Knitting Patterns.* New York: Charles Scribners Sons, 1970 (BWII); *A Treasury of Knitting Patterns.* New York: Charles Scribner's Sons, 1968 (BWI).

Aran cardigan with Fibonacci panels

I always begin an Aran by looking through all my stitch pattern books that include cables, particularly Gladys Thompson and all three volumes by Barbara Walker (see Further reading at left).

Basics—This sweater is done in worsted-weight two-ply handspun Cotswald (but any worsted weight will do). For a heavy, tightly knit jacket, I choose the smallest needle size (2 and 4) that will allow me to turn the cables. The *gauge* will be variable. You should knit swatches for all possible patterns and combine those that produce panels of the desired widths. To fit a 36 in. bust as a loose jacket, the sweater is 41 in. around. (See the drawing at right for dimensions of the pieces.)

Calculating panels—Beginning with the back, I decide to divide the 20-in. piece into a central panel and mirror-image cable strips according to a slightly rearranged Fibonacci series—1,2,3,1,5,1,3,2,1,—figuring to make up the 1-in. difference in pattern adjustments.

I start swatching patterns. Ideally, my cables will all be some multiple of four sts wide and four rows between repeats. Gladys Thompson's tree and diamond twist-stitch pattern works out to 5 in. wide on size 4 needles, perfect for my center panel since it is the fifth Fibonacci number. To achieve the sense of a 7½ in. central panel, I find a 1¼-in. "OXO" cable to place on either side. Many classic Arans have a narrow, complex-looking braid on each edge: Barbara Walker's "Aran braid" is only slightly over 1 in. wide (especially when I substitute my first twist-stitch divider for one of its background stitches). After knitting a multitude of samples, I find an assortment of 1 in., 2 in., and 3 in. patterns that meet all my criteria, and I lay out the patterns for related but different front and

Aran calculations

back panels as shown in the drawing at right.

A single twist stitch separates cables with similar relief, so I place one between every panel, excluding the central three. Now the width is up to 20 in. To assure the mirror-image symmetry of the pretzel braid on the right and left sides, I begin the first one at row 1 and the second at row 17 (half way up the pattern). Very little fudging on the length of the piece allows all cables to end at a complete multiple (or a half-repeat). The front, observing the same multiples, will work out evenly too.

Cardigan issues—Since this is a cardigan, I split the center tree and diamond panel, putting the same central stitch of the panel on each center front edge, and I let the ribbing continue up the center fronts in pattern. In order not to disturb the ribbed band, all increases will be made in the pattern stitches after these first 8 sts.

I am ready to count stitches for the pattern and rib. Because the Aran has 30% more stitches than a stockinette sweater of the same size, I can't use the usual 10% less for ribbing. Instead, I'll cast on about 30% fewer stitches and knit the ribbing on needles two sizes smaller. A row of purl on a right side row, with the small needles at the top of the rib where I increase to the body patterns, will minimize the flare that so many additional stitches are likely to produce.

I always knit both fronts at the same time. For a cardigan, you must space buttonholes evenly up the right front (for women). Don't forget to place a buttonhole at the lower edge and at the top of the rib. You also need a hole at the top of the body and in the neck rib. All others should be evenly spaced along the length of the front.

Sleeves—Traditional Arans often employ a shoulder saddle (approximately 3 or 4 in. wide). I use my 3 in. symmetrical braid in the center and place the "Aran braid" on either side with a twisted stitch in between. I add about an inch of moss stitch on each edge. Since I want a very full jacket, I also knit separate 8-in. long diamond-shaped gussets to be sewn in under the arms. See the drawing at right for details. □

Front (in inches)

1½	T	2	T	3	T	1	2½	1	1	2½	1	T	3	T	2	T	1½
Relief		Twist		Relief		Relief	Twist	Ribs		Twist	Relief		Relief		Twist		Relief
Aran braid (BWII*)		Ribbed cable (BWI)		Branching braid (BWIII)		Scotch faggoting (BWI)	Tree and diamond (GT)			Tree and diamond (GT)	Scotch faggoting (BWI)		Branching braid (BWIII)		Ribbed cable (BWI)		Aran braid (BWII)
Stitches																	
11	1	11	1	24	1	8	18	8	8	18	8	1	24	1	11	1	11

*See further reading for pattern references.

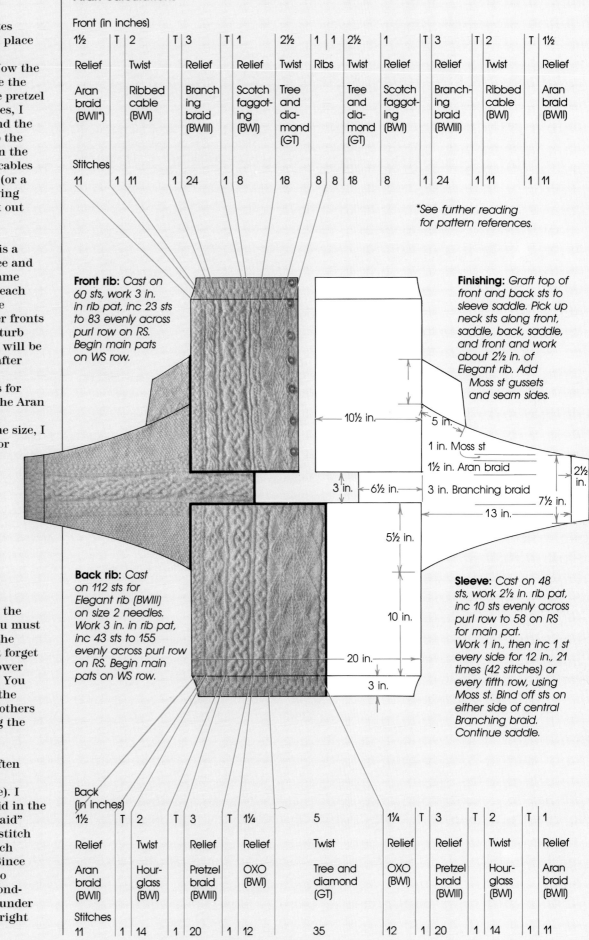

Front rib: Cast on 60 sts, work 3 in. in rib pat, inc 23 sts to 83 evenly across purl row on RS. Begin main pats on WS row.

Back rib: Cast on 112 sts for Elegant rib (BWIII) on size 2 needles. Work 3 in. in rib pat, inc 43 sts to 155 evenly across purl row on RS. Begin main pats on WS row.

Finishing: Graft top of front and back sts to sleeve saddle. Pick up neck sts along front, saddle, back, saddle, and front and work about 2½ in. of Elegant rib. Add Moss st gussets and seam sides.

10½ in. 5 in. 1 in. Moss st 1½ in. Aran braid 3 in. Branching braid 7½ in. 2½ in. 3 in. 6½ in. 13 in. 5½ in. 10 in. 20 in. 3 in.

Sleeve: Cast on 48 sts, work 2½ in. rib pat, inc 10 sts evenly across purl row to 58 on RS for main pat. Work 1 in., then inc 1 st every side for 12 in., 21 times (42 stitches) or every fifth row, using Moss st. Bind off sts on either side of central Branching braid. Continue saddle.

Back (in inches)

1½	T	2	T	3	T	1¼	5	1¼	T	3	T	2	T	1
Relief		Twist		Relief		Relief	Twist	Relief		Relief		Twist		Relief
Aran braid (BWII)		Hourglass (BWI)		Pretzel braid (BWIII)		OXO (BWI)	Tree and diamond (GT)	OXO (BWI)		Pretzel braid (BWIII)		Hourglass (BWI)		Aran braid (BWII)
Stitches														
11	1	14	1	20	1	12	35	12	1	20	1	14	1	11

Knitting Sideways

Increase your garment design options and reduce the number of seams at the same time

by Molly Geissman

I've loved to knit since I was young. I've especially enjoyed the endless creative possibilities for fabric design that knitting offers. But there is one aspect of making a sweater I've always disliked: sewing the seams with yarn and a tapestry needle. In early years, to keep me knitting, my mother sewed all the seams for me.

I'm still knitting and, in fact, now make my living designing and knitting sweaters and selling yarn. And I've found a way to avoid sewing so many seams: I knit all my sweaters sideways from cuff to cuff, instead of from bottom to top, so the knitted rows run up and down rather than around the body.

Each sweater can be knitted in one or two large pieces, which reduces the number of seams that need to be joined. There are no armhole or shoulder seams with drop-shoulder styling, which makes for a softer, less structured garment. Only the side/sleeve seams need joining. You can knit the garment entirely flat, working back and forth on long circular needles, as I did with the sweater at right. Or, if the sleeves aren't shaped in steps, you can knit them in the round to eliminate another pair of seams, and work the body flat. Whichever approach you take, construct the edges so you can *knit* the seams together, as I'll explain a little later.

Knitting sweaters sideways offers design advantages as well. You can create a fabric with a pattern running continuously from front to back and from wrist to wrist uninterrupted by shoulder or armhole seams. Conventionally knitted, horizontal stripes and pattern bands tend to make the wearer appear wider than she or he is. But the same stripes become complimentary—and look updated—when they run vertically on the body.

Since the rows stack vertically in a sweater knitted sideways, the designs tend to flow vertically. This means that you can make the focal point of the garment the center front to flatter the face, or widen the focus by moving it out towards the shoulders.

Sideways vs. traditional knitting

The drawing on p. 46 will guide you through knitting a sweater sideways. Before you start, however, there are some important characteristics to be aware of, including gauge and fabric stretch.

Gauge in sideways knitting—Applying a sample swatch's stitch and row gauge measurements to a sweater takes on new meaning in sideways knitting. You'll use the rows/in. gauge to determine the garment's width (not the length, as in conventional knitting) and the sts./in. gauge to arrive at the length. The most important gauge is the sts./in. because there's more give between stitches than between rows, which can cause the fabric to stretch lengthwise. You can control the extra stretch by the stitch pattern, fiber, and knitting technique you choose.

I usually knit my sweaters in stockinette stitch (knitting every row on the right side of the garment and purling each row on the wrong side). Because open, lacy patterns tend to stretch much more than stockinette, I don't recommend them for sideways knitting. For any stitch pattern, plain or fancy, you can check the stretch by knitting, dressing, and hanging a sample swatch (see *Threads* No. 51, pp. 59-61) with the stitches placed sideways.

The fiber you use plays a role in how much the sweater will stretch. Wool has a wonderful ability to bounce back from being stretched, but silk and cotton have considerably less memory. This doesn't mean you can't use silk or cotton. But I recommend a yarn that's a blend of silk or cotton and wool so the yarn has some resilience. Or you can knit with two strands of yarn at once, one of silk or cotton and one of wool. (One strand of fingering weight with one of sport-weight yarn approximates a worsted-weight yarn.)

Another way to compensate for stretch is to plan your sweater an inch or two shorter than normal. You can also add stability by knitting with two colors per row, carrying the unused yarn in floats across the back. This stranded knitting, called Fair Isle, helps hold the fabric together and reduces stretching.

When knitted sideways, the fabric will also have less flexibility in the width. To

Stripes take on a different look when they run vertically. *This sweater was knitted flat from cuff to center in a pattern mimicking an African fabric (shown above right). The side and center-back seams (see inset at right) were knitted together and cast off, while the sleeve seams were joined and corded in one step.*

How to knit a sweater sideways

You can knit this sweater in one large piece from the right cuff to the left cuff, as described in steps 1-9. Or knit in two halves as I did: Knit one half from right cuff to center front and back, placing back stitches on a holder. Then knit a second half from wrist to center, reversing shaping. After knitting, join the center-back stitches by knitting the seam together. Use the same technique to join side seams that were started with stranded, or open-edge, cast-on (see *Threads*, No. 55, p. 20).

Note: Unless otherwise specified, use long-tail cast-on (see *Threads* No. 54, p. 20).

1. Cuff. Cast on sts for cuff hem or ribbing; work flat.

2. Sleeve shaping. Using a separate length of yarn, cast on required number of sts when you reach a step.

3. Right body. Using open-edge cast-on, add sts at each end of sleeve for front and back body, placing marker at center shoulder. (To determine number of sts, subtract half sleeve sts from total sts needed to span measurement from shoulder to hem.) Knit body to right side of neck opening. At the same time, shape lower edges by casting on at each end. Place back sts on a separate needle or holder.

4. Right front. Work right front sts, binding off on left side to shape neck opening. At center front, you can change to a ribbing or hem pattern to make button band or place stitches on a holder and add trim later.

5. Left front. Cast on sts (matching number in right front) and knit ribbing or hem for left front band, or cast on invisibly for addition of trim later. Knit left front, casting on sts at left edge for neck shaping to match right front. Leave sts on holder or needle.

6. Back. Work back sts from separate needle or holder across to left neck edge, shaping back neck if desired. Number of rows should match that of the fronts, excluding trim or ribbing.

7. Left body. With fronts and back complete to left side of neck opening, join front to back by knitting all sts onto one needle, starting at hem, knitting to shoulder, and continuing to hem on opposite side. Knit same number of rows as in right body, reversing lower edge shaping by binding off sts.

8. Left sleeve. Place side sts of body on holders or hold with stranded cast-off and continue on sleeve stitches. Reverse shaping by binding off as you reach a step. Finish with hem or ribbing and bind off loosely.

9. Finishing. Join sleeve underarm seam using a 3-st knitted cord (see *Threads*, No. 55, p. 22). *Lower edge:* work 3-st knitted cord around entire edge. *Neck:* Pick up and knit ribbed collar, then work 3-st cord along outline of neck.

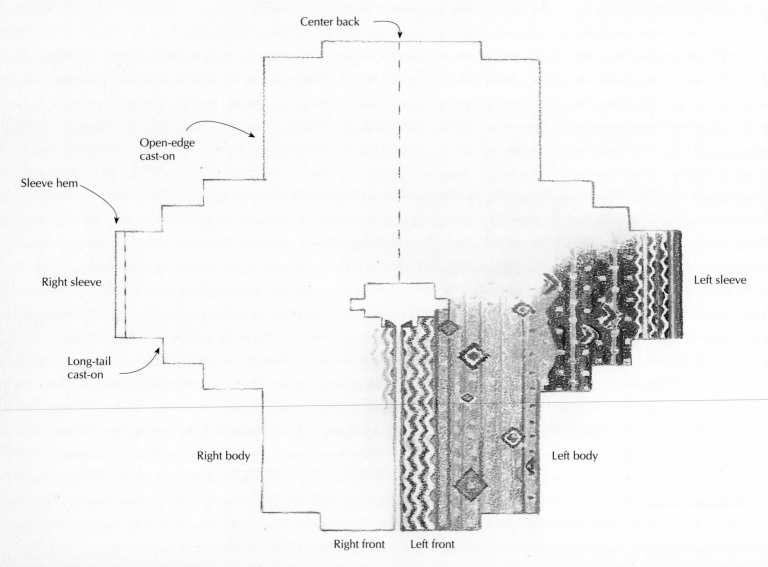

Center back

Open-edge cast-on

Sleeve hem

Right sleeve

Long-tail cast-on

Right body

Right front

Left front

Left sleeve

Left body

compensate, I add 1 to 3 in. more ease than normal, depending on the fiber I'm using. Thicker and nonwool fibers require more ease than do sport-weight wools.

Knitted seams help the garment hang evenly—The side seams and opening edges of sweaters knitted sideways fall along rows of stitches, rather than on the selvage stitches.

If I cast on stitches on one side and bind them off on the other before seaming them together, the sweater will hang lopsided. This is because cast-on stitches have more give than bound-off stitches.

To avoid this, I don't cast on and off in the usual way. I use the stranded, or open-edge, cast-on to add stitches, which are held on a strand of yarn. And when a section is complete, I place the stitches on a holder or use the stranded cast-off. When I'm ready to join the seam, I place the open stitches on needles, and knit and cast off the two sets of live stitches together. This produces a straight, flat seam and makes the two sides of the garment hang evenly.

Needles you'll need

In general, sideways knitting requires more needles than regular horizontal knitting. If your circular needle isn't long enough to hold all the stitches for the

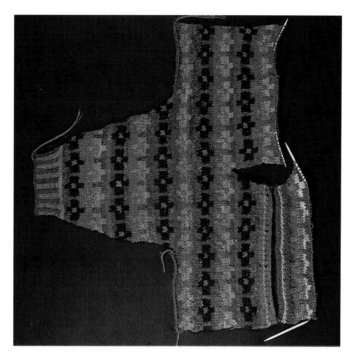

Halfway done: The right half of this sweater uses the open-edge cast-on to hold the stitches at the sides. Ribbing finishes the center-front edges, and the left front piece is ready to join to the back.

front and back of an adult sweater, knit with two circular needles of the same size. To knit an adult cardigan working the sleeves flat, as shown in the photo above, you'll need one or two 24- or 31-in. circular needles for knitting the sleeves and body. In addition, you'll need one 24-in. circular needle two sizes smaller for knitting the ribbing at the bottom, front

edges, and neck. To knit the same cardigan working the sleeves in the round, you'll also need a set of four double-pointed needles in both body and ribbing sizes and a 16-in. circular needle in the body size for the sleeves.

As you might imagine, knitting a sweater in one piece can make for a large, bulky bunch of fabric in your lap. To reduce the

Knitting Fair Isle sideways

by Kate Barber

Years ago, I knitted my first traditional Fair Isle vest in the round, complete with steeks, or knitted sections that are cut open for the armholes, front opening, and neck (see *Threads* No. 50, pp. 20, 22). Knitting a tube makes stranded colors very easy to work with, but I wanted to get away from Fair Isle's traditional horizontal patterning. By simply shifting the orientation of the knitted tube sideways, I found that garments made with these traditional patterns take on an entirely different look.

Because these patterns will be viewed vertically rather than horizontally, they may look quite different than you expect. As a result, swatching is crucial.

The vests I make—all with yarns I spin and then dye—

usually end at or above the waist, but you can certainly make a longer vest. Just remember that the longer the vest, the larger the tube's circumference

must be.

After knitting the tube, turn it on its side for finishing. The armholes and neck can be cut open in several ways, as shown in

the drawing below, and the bottom edge of the tube will be cut along its entire length. Although it's not traditional to do so, I suggest machine stitching just ⇨

Knitting a Fair Isle vest sideways

After knitting a tube, turn it sideways and decide how you want to cut the neck and armholes. Sew just inside the cutting lines for the neck, armholes, front opening, and bottom edge. Cut the openings, and finish the cut edges.

Knitting direction

Front opening

Knitted steek or cutting line

Knitted tube

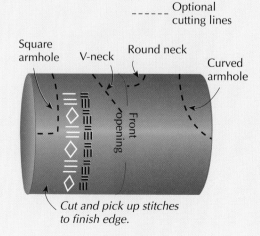

Optional cutting lines

Square armhole

V-neck

Round neck

Curved armhole

Front opening

Cut and pick up stitches to finish edge.

Tube turned sideways

Illustrations by Carla Ruzicka

bulk, I now usually knit sweaters in two halves and join them with a knitted seam at the center back, as described on p. 46. Splitting the knitting also makes it easier to knit two identically patterned pieces; once I make the right half, I refer to it for the pattern while reversing the shaping to make the left half.

Design ideas

One of the most exciting aspects of knitting this way is creating and developing a design. I am passionately drawn to the color and geometric motifs found in ethnic textiles from Africa, the Middle East, and Central and South America, as well as from Native American tribes. These cultures generally produce woven textiles, whose structure is, of course, very different from knitted fabric. But I find it very exciting to adapt woven designs for knitted wearables.

I may adapt a design as a whole, or I may take only an element of it to use variously throughout my garment design, as, for example, with the diamonds and vertical zigzagging rows in the sweater on p. 45. I may even extend the imagery to the sleeve, neck, or hem shaping, as I did with the zigzag-inspired stepped edge on the same sweater.

I begin to work out a design by referring to an actual textile or a photo of an artifact or design that I like, such as a kilim rug. I place the design lines sideways so they run vertically on the body. If I want to check the size or number of stitches needed for a particular motif, I'll sketch or work it out on knitters' graph paper. Often, however, I'll dive right in and, with my inspirational artifact or image nearby for reference, design as I knit.

Designing as you knit is fun and not nearly as hard as it sounds. If you want a symmetrical design, begin to duplicate the design in reverse after you reach the center (or knit the sweater in two halves). If you want an asymmetrical design, you can design as you knit throughout, but be sure that both sides of the garment are visually balanced, whether with the imagery itself or with color and/or texture.

Construction

The sweater on p. 45 was inspired by a piece of African cloth from Bakuba, Zaire. It was knitted using both Fair Isle and intarsia techniques, as shown in the drawing sequence on p. 46. The diamond motifs were done with intarsia, while the striped background was stranded across the diamond motifs throughout.

The beauty of finishing a jacket like this is that it requires no sewing except for whipstitching the facing of the front bands. (I work a row of purl stitches at the center of the double-width band to create a fold line.) The side seams are knitted together and bound off at the same time, and the sleeve seams are joined by knitting them together with a three-stitch cord.

Finally, I pick up stitches along the neck for the collar if the design calls for one, and along the bottom if I'm using ribbing. (I usually subtract about 10 to 20 percent of the total number of rows around the garment to arrive at the number of stitches to pick up.) And because sweaters knitted sideways have a soft, unstructured fit and dropped shoulders, they would benefit from the added definition of knitted shoulder pads, which are simple to make (see *Threads* No. 55, p. 22).

I've been teaching sideways knitting for five years, and I find that many people have a hard time visualizing this process the first time through. It may help to knit a doll-size sample first to firmly establish the steps in your mind. Sketching an "aerial view" may also help, since that's how the garment will look as you knit it. Once you get going, I think you'll see how easy the process is. ☐

Molly Geissman is an owner of Village Wools in Albuquerque, NM, where she teaches knitting and designs sweaters.

(continued from p. 47) inside the cutting line to reduce raveling.

Finishing the cut bottom edge, armholes, and neck is probably the most demanding part of making such a garment, but I find it the most exciting step since there are lots of options to choose from. Among the simplest ways to finish a cut edge is to bind it, as you would woven fabric, with bias tape or ribbon. You can also cover the edge with corded or braided trim that you buy or make. To make trim using the same yarns as those in the vest, try card-weaving bands (see *Threads* No. 31, pp. 52-55).

You might also take inspiration from traditional Scandinavian sweaters and cover the cut edges with felt or fabric, embroider the bands, and use silver frog closures. Or crochet the edge with lace, Tunisian crochet, or a tight single-crochet stitch worked for several rows then finished with a backwards single crochet.

Finally, a knitted-on band and facing, which I used on the neck, armhole, and bottom edges of the vest at left, makes a wonderful finish. (The front band and facing were knitted in the round with stitches picked up on the front and back of each front edge. When the band and facing were the width I wanted, I knitted the "front" and "back" stitches off together to finish the front band.)

To prevent a knitted-on band from flaring out, pick up about 10 percent fewer stitches than found in the edge being covered (if the band is more than ¾ in. wide or is narrower but still seems to need pulling in, decrease the stitches by another 10 percent on a subsequent row). For a flat band and facing that cup the edge they cover, work the band in reverse stockinette and the facing in stockinette. (For a fuller band, like that on the sleeve openings of the vest at left, work the band in garter stitch and use stockinette stitch for the facing.) Finally, instead of binding off the stitches, whipstitch the live stitches to secure the band in place.

Kate Barber spins, dyes, and knits in Seattle, WA.

Cutting a vest from a knitted tube gives you freedom to choose neck, armhole, and front shaping later.

A Patterning Primer for Custom Knitting

You can easily create geometric designs to embellish any simple sweater

by Nancy Bush

as a knitwear designer, I've been inspired by the many pattern possibilities to be found in my native Utah. Here in the Southwest, I've explored the many museums, galleries, and shops specializing in Native American patterned pottery, rugs, and other crafts. A design file bulges with pictures, postcards, and photocopies of patterns that I encounter.

I've been able to incorporate many of these patterns into my sweater designs. These patterns are often easy to chart and offer an endless supply of inspiration for knitted fabrics.

Even if you've never charted a pattern before, you'll find geometric patterns an easy place to start. It's helpful to learn how to draw on graph paper. With the few simple rules for charting that I follow, you'll advance from drawing simple lines to capturing more complex shapes.

With patterns in hand, you're ready to plot them onto a simple sweater shape. When designing with geometric patterns, I've found that an unfussy sweater shape helps them to look their best. A basic, boxy pullover, like the one I describe on pp. 52-53, is a perfect choice because it

The simple, boxy shape of this traditional Norwegian pullover is a perfect showplace for easy-to-chart geometric patterns.

From *Threads* magazine (December 1993) 50:51-55

Photo by Susan Kahn

Charting patterns on graph paper

When capturing a geometric pattern on paper, it's often easier to draw a single pattern unit first. You can then repeat this unit to form the larger pattern.

As you learn to chart, you'll find there are many ways to chart a shape. Stripes and dots can vary in width and size. Small shapes can be filled to form solid areas. Larger shapes can be created from groups of diagonal lines.

Key to symbols

On graph paper, each square represents a stitch; each horizontal line of squares represents a row of knitted stitches. Use an X to indicate a pattern stitch and an open square to show background

Step-by-step charting

1. Identify a pattern unit, or a portion, from a geometric design.
2. Starting at a single square, decide the direction of your first line(s).
3. Draw X's in the direction of your line(s). "X" across for a horizontal line, or upwards for a vertical line. For a diagonal line, "X" upwards or downwards in the direction of the adjacent corner. "X" additional lines to complete the unit.
4. Repeat unit at sides and/or above to see how they connect. If necessary, leave a space between units, or merge them by eliminating an X where units meet.
5. Design small units to fill empty spaces. For instance, a small diamond or triangle could be placed between larger motifs.
6. Mark lines where pattern begins and ends a repeat.

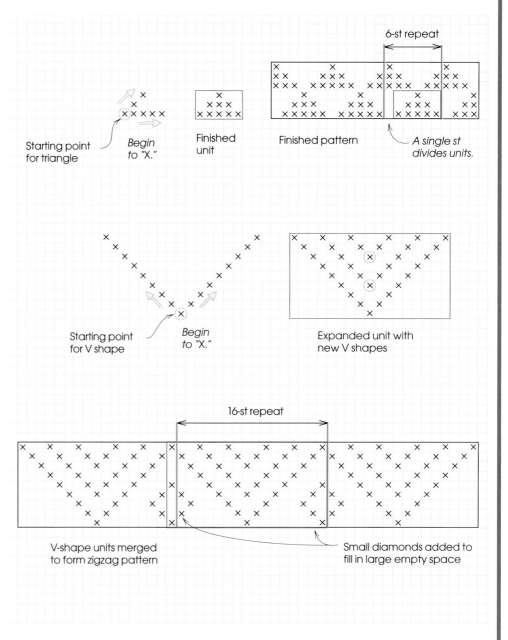

Starting point for triangle — Begin to "X." — Finished unit — Finished pattern — A single st divides units.

Starting point for V shape — Begin to "X." — Expanded unit with new V shapes

6-st repeat

16-st repeat

V-shape units merged to form zigzag pattern — Small diamonds added to fill in large empty space

is boxy and virtually unshaped. Patterns sit neatly on its surface, without awkward interruptions.

Learning to place patterns for the best visual effect is the last step before the pleasure of actually knitting your sweater. I've found that with geometric patterns and a simple sweater, even a novice can achieve success.

Capturing patterns on paper

Many ethnic crafts feature geometric patterns that are easy to adapt to knitting. The small triangle pattern in my sweater on p. 49 came from a painted floorcloth. The featherlike yoke pattern was inspired by a Coalmine Mesa carpet. You can also find designs in Turkish kilim rugs, African textiles, or Greek embroidery, to name a few.

Choosing a pattern—I look for patterns that lend themselves to using only two colors on a row. Most knitters find it easier to carry only two yarns (see *Threads* No. 50, p. 20), one for the background and one for the contrasting pattern. If I do need a third color, I find it easier to duplicate stitch it into the finished knitting if it is not used extensively.

I also look for patterns formed of stripes, triangles, diamonds, and zigzags. Most of these can be composed with diagonal lines. Also, geometric patterns with an obvious repeat are the easiest to translate. Since I am a firm believer in low-stress knitting, I avoid irregular patterns that are less repetitive because they are harder to knit. I keep the scale of my patterns fairly small, and I try never to have more than 5 sts between color changes so the yarn being carried won't form long floats. If my pattern has open sections, I try to fill in these spaces with small pattern units, so I won't have to carry yarn over long stretches.

Guidelines for charting—I generally use 10- by 10-in. square graph paper designed by Keuffel and Esser (available at art- or drafting-supply stores). This paper has green lines which photocopy well and can be used for charting larger sections of a sweater as well as small patterns. You can use any other size square grid paper. While the square grid doesn't have the relationship to knitted stitches of knitters' proportioned graph paper, I find it well suited to geometric patterns. To test the look of your patterns, and to find out what your gauge is, you'll need to swatch a pattern.

It's a good idea to practice drawing patterns on graph paper (for examples, see the drawings on the facing page). For a simple horizontal stripe, simply draw X's across a row; for a vertical stripe, "X" upwards. To make a heavier stripe, increase the width to two or more stitches. To capture more complicated shapes on paper, I begin by analyzing the basic shapes that form the pattern. After a while, charting becomes second nature, but in the beginning it's useful to break down a pattern into smaller pieces. Is the basic unit a zigzag, a triangle, or a maybe a diamond? If there is a unit that repeats, chart that unit first.

The last thing you'll have to do with a finished pattern is mark the repeat lines to show the small segment of pattern that, when repeated, forms the larger allover pattern. First draw a vertical line at some point in the patterning. For ease, choose a point at the beginning of an obvious shape or motif. Count over in one direction until the shape repeats again. Draw another vertical line to enclose the segment that forms the pattern. For your reference, write in the number of stitches that forms the repeat.

Choosing a simple sweater

After you have assembled some designs you like, then you need to find a basic sweater pattern onto which you can plot them. Choose a sweater pattern that has no complicated shaping at armhole and neckline. Dropped-shoulder sweaters or boat-neck pullovers provide clean, sharp lines that suit geometric designs. A sweater with more shaping, like a raglan, will often cut into your designs in an unsightly way. If you are unsure of size, refer to a sweater pattern that you know fits you well.

I have had great success placing patterns on the traditional Norwegian sweater. This easy-to-knit pullover is boxy and un-

shaped, except for a rounded front neckline. The sweater has separate areas that lend themselves to certain kinds of patterning. I placed a hemmed border on the sweater shown on p. 49, but you could work a ribbing instead. Above this is a good place for a small repetitive pattern. Because the sweater is circular-knit, you can make the pattern continuous in this section, with no breaks. The prominent yoke section is a focal point for placing your most attractive pattern. Since the yoke is interrupted by openings for armholes and placket front, the pattern doesn't have to be continuous. You can place a larger, more isolated pattern here if you wish. The front yoke can also be different from the back yoke.

Norwegian sweaters have a few other characteristics that make them good canvases for geometric patterns. Pattern knitting is easy in the round, as the right side of the fabric is always facing you. Openings for armholes and placket front are cut from the circular tube of knitting. To make this easier, a small space at the base of each opening is bound off during the knitting. Then, on the next round, a bridge of knitting, called a *steek*, is cast on. This connecting piece of fabric, about 1 in. wide, is then knit up to the shoulder. To cut the openings, the steek areas are first reinforced by machine stitching,

> *I try never to have more than five stitches between color changes so the yarn being carried won't form long floats.*

then cut open to form armhole and placket openings. This may sound intimidating, but it's actually quite easy if you proceed step by step. If you've never tried knitting this kind of sweater before, refer to *Threads* No. 50, pp. 20-22.

Swatching

To see the knit version of your patterns and also to provide a gauge swatch, you'll need to swatch first in the yarn that you've chosen. Yarn weight affects how your patterns look. When designing for the Norwegian pullover, I've had success working with sport-weight wool. With a fairly fine gauge of 6 sts/in., this yarn keeps my patterns small and neat, which I like. If I were to use a heavier yarn, my

patterns would have a larger scale.

If you are planning a sweater in pieces, you'll knit a swatch back and forth. But if you are planning a circular-knit sweater, you must knit a circular swatch to get a true gauge for your fabric; a swatch knit back and forth may yield a slightly different gauge than a swatch knit in the round.

There are two ways to knit a circular swatch. You can cast on and knit in the round on a small 16- or 20-in. circular needle. This creates a large swatch; however, after measuring gauge, you can rip out this swatch to reuse the yarn. Or, you can knit a smaller swatch by using circular needles as you would straight ones and knitting only right-side rows. Cast on with a circular needle, and knit a row; cut the yarn, slip the stitches back to the beginning of the needle, rejoin yarn, and repeat. This takes less time, but you cannot reuse the yarn.

Fitting patterns into a basic sweater

Whether you knit your sweater in pieces or in the round, you'll encounter several different situations for plotting patterns. Often a pattern needs to fit exactly. Sometimes a pattern won't fit exactly and you'll have to center it. Other times a pattern needs to be isolated.

After you have made your swatch, estimate approximately how many stitches you will need for any section or piece (see *Threads* No. 50, p. 22). Keep in mind that, in most cases, you will need to adjust these numbers to accommodate your patterns. For example, you may need a few more or less stitches in any section to make a pattern fit exactly. You'll also need to refer to your pattern repeat. I find it easier to add a few stitches to a piece than to adjust the pattern.

An exact fit—Sometimes you'll need to make a pattern fit exactly, as in a circular-knit piece where a pattern is to be continuous. In my sweater, I used the small triangle pattern in this way. If your pattern repeat divides evenly into your desired number of stitches, simply begin the pattern at the beginning of the round or piece and repeat to the end. If your pattern repeat doesn't divide evenly, add or subtract a few stitches to make it fit ex-

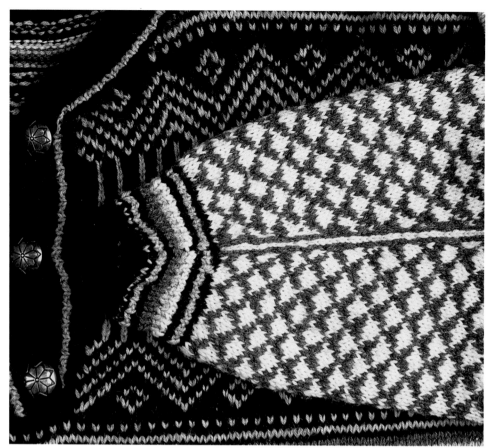

When a pattern, such as the triangles in the sleeve above, doesn't fit an area exactly, a line of stitches that mimics a seam eliminates an awkward merging of patterns. This line adds a sense of order and symmetry.

Knitting a basic pullover on a circular needle

If you'd like to make a circular-knit Norwegian sweater with cut armholes and placket front like the one shown on p. 49, you can use this schematic as a guideline for shape and general measurements. It shows a medium-size woman's sweater with a slightly loose fit, knit in sport-weight yarn. Compare these measurements to a sweater that fits you well, and adjust accordingly. Also, if you plan to use a heavier yarn, add 2 to 4 in. to the body to accommodate extra bulk.

To judge how many stitches you'll need, refer to your gauge swatch (how many sts/in. and rows/in.—see *Threads* No. 50, p. 22). When placing patterns in different sections, you may need to adjust your stitch counts to accommodate pattern size or repeats.

After planning, here's a basic process to follow to knit the sweater. The entire sweater, except for the neck, is knit in the round with right side facing.
A. For body, cast on and place marker for beg of round at one side.
B. Knit ribbing or border and lower body section.
C. At beg of each armhole and placket, allot 1 in. of sts to be worked plain or as a steek to be cut later for armhole opening.
D. At neck edge, bind off placket steek sts.
E. To shape neck edge, work back and forth, not circular, binding off gradually (for more on shaping a front neck, see *Threads* No. 45, p.55).
F. At shoulder, bind off armhole steeks, then slip sts for each shoulder and back neck to holders.
G. Cut steeks.
H. Join shoulders together by bind-off method (see *Threads* No. 50, p. 22).
I. For a sleeve started at the cuff, cast on and place marker for beg of round. Knit ribbing.
J. Above rib, mark 1 st at beg of round as seam st. Keeping in pat, gradually inc before and after seam st until sleeve is twice armhole depth.
K. Sew sleeves to body. Pick up sts and knit edgings at neck and placket.

actly, as long as this won't spoil the fit of your garment. Small patterns are useful in large areas since adding or subtracting a few stitches rarely makes a difference in fit. I almost always add stitches because a slightly larger sweater is easier to wear than a smaller one.

Centering a pattern—Often a pattern will be too large to fit exactly, and adding or subtracting will affect fit adversely. For a flat piece, calculate how many full pattern repeats will fit, then divide the partial repeat stitches in half, and place them to either side. This creates a symmetry within the pattern. For a circular piece, I prefer to set up one or more seam stitches at the sides of the body section. To make them stand out as divider lines, I work these stitches in purl or in a solid color. Then I treat both front and back as separate sections. I like the patterns to create a mirror image at the sides where they meet the seam stitches for balance.

I also make a seam stitch on my circular-knit sleeves above the ribbing (see the photo above). The seam stitch acts as a divider line, allowing the pattern to begin and end cleanly, and it makes working the pattern easier as I increase before and after it to shape the sleeve.

Isolating a pattern—You can isolate a pattern section on a separate piece or smaller section, such as the yoke of a circular-knit sweater. Decide how large your section is, then plot the pattern section within the confines of this space, leaving an unpatterned section at the edges, as I did at the sides of the yoke. I charted the whole sweater yoke so that I'd have something to follow during the knitting.

Making adjustments—When making the transition from lower body of a Norwegian sweater to the yoke, you may find that the number of stitches in the lower body is not the number you need to place your patterns in the yoke. It's fine to add or subtract a few evenly spaced stitches between these two sections, as this will not really affect fit.

Lastly, if your patterns don't fit into a given space, you can always go back to your chart and alter it. As I often do, you may find that you'll devise a new pattern in the process! □

Nancy Bush owns The Wooly West yarn store in Salt Lake City, and is a free-lance knitwear designer and knitting teacher. She designs regularly for Knitters *magazine and several yarn companies.*

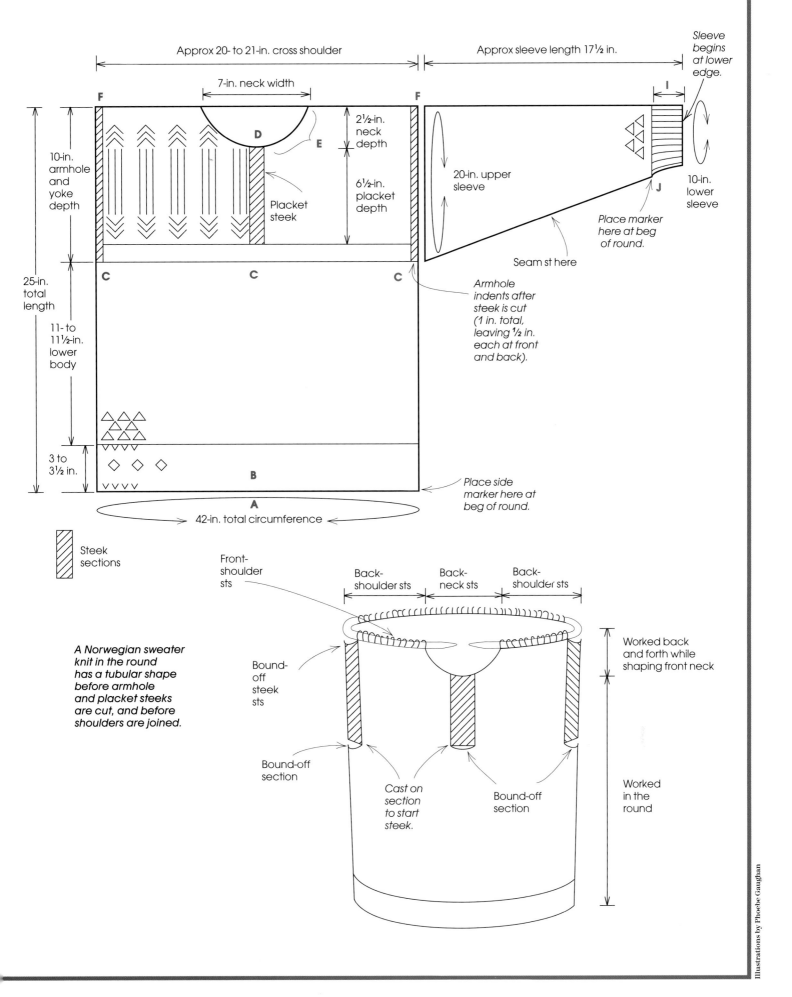

Approx 20- to 21-in. cross shoulder

Approx sleeve length 17½ in.

Sleeve begins at lower edge.

7-in. neck width

F   F   I

10-in. armhole and yoke depth

D

E

2½-in. neck depth

6½-in. placket depth

Placket steek

20-in. upper sleeve

10-in. lower sleeve

J

Place marker here at beg of round.

25-in. total length

C   C   C

Armhole indents after steek is cut (1 in. total, leaving ½ in. each at front and back).

Seam st here

11- to 11½-in. lower body

3 to 3½ in.

B

Place side marker here at beg of round.

A

42-in. total circumference

Steek sections

A Norwegian sweater knit in the round has a tubular shape before armhole and placket steeks are cut, and before shoulders are joined.

Front-shoulder sts

Back-shoulder sts

Back-neck sts

Back-shoulder sts

Worked back and forth while shaping front neck

Bound-off steek sts

Bound-off section

Cast on section to start steek.

Bound-off section

Worked in the round

Subtle Color Shading for Patterned Knits

You can paint a knit fabric, then unravel and reknit for smooth color transitions

by Rebekah Younger

aybe you think I'm crazy to knit a fabric, unravel the yarn, and knit it again. No, it's not because I drop stitches; I do it on purpose. You see, my goal is to create a Fair Isle or patterned knit with colors that shade smoothly through both the main and contrast yarns—smoother and more subtle shading than I can get by knitting with many close shades of yarn (which leaves abrupt lines between colors and dozens of yarn ends to work in).

The way I produce this subtle shading is first to knit two undyed rectangles of fabric for each garment section—one for the main yarn, one for the contrast yarn. Then I paint them with textile dye, blending and shading the colors right on the fabric. When the fabric is dry, I unravel the yarn into two balls and knit the pattern I want.

Watching the way colors blend in nature, particularly in the stunning California sunsets, sparked my desire for shading in my knits. What intrigues me is how seldom colors clash in nature. Blending disparate shades to make a third compatible shade gives a subtle transition that ties the colors together. Admittedly, knitting twice is less daunting by machine than by hand; a machine

knitter can knit a large square of plain stockinette in a matter of minutes and, with a ball winder, unravel in even less time. But even hand knitters can find this process satisfying: Start by using painted yarn in a small garment section such as a collar, cuffs, or an inset like the one shown on p. 57.

Experiment with color

Before starting to work with paint and yarn, experiment with color by drawing on graph paper with colored pencils, overlapping colors as you change pencils. Or use a computer and a paint program with a gradient color feature, such as Deluxe Paint III (available for IBM or Macintosh). Either approach allows you to preview quickly a variety of color options without knitting and painting a lot of different swatches.

To achieve shading both in the pattern and background of a Fair Isle design, use one range of colors for the pattern, then a second range for the background. Color ranges may start light and blend to darker shades (as in a sunset) or work in opposite directions, with one color range cool and the other warm, like the chart and knitted inset on p. 57. The options are endless. Strong contrast, such as a yellow-to-orange range knitted with a purple-to-blue one, makes the colors really sing. I never tire of the moment of discovery, finding out which colors lie next to each other when I knit the two yarns together. Even with all the planning, there is still an element of chance determining which shade will lie next to another.

From *Threads* magazine (June 1995) 59:68-71

Yarns and dyes that work

To get the color effects I want, I use a combination of yarn, dye, and techniques that I've worked out by trial and error. Experiment on swatches to discover wonderful effects with other yarns and dyes.

The benefits of knitting with silk—I choose silk yarn for my painted garments for several reasons. It has a sheen and color saturation unparalleled by other fibers. It dyes easily without the need for dye pots or a stove, which I'll discuss later. And, above all, it's a strong, resilient fiber that withstands the process of knitting, wetting, dyeing, fixing the dye, unraveling, and reknitting without dramatic shifts in gauge and without felting. I often use the natural spun silk yarn called Cascade from Henry's Attic (available from Village Wools, 3801 San Mateo Blvd. NE, Albuquerque, NM 87106; 505-883-2919), as well as the Tussah slubby

steam setting. Dharma sells these dyes and Dyeset, and their free catalog has accessories for dyeing plus valuable information on techniques.

How much to knit?

The trickiest part of my knit/paint process is determining how much of each color group to knit. Calculating the exact amounts is a bit of a hassle. You don't *have* to estimate it accurately, but I do it both to economize on silk and so I can predict fairly precisely where the colors will appear in the finished garment.

If you decide to try the paint process for only a small area, rather than a full garment, you can skip the calculations and simply paint some extra yarn. Knit two stockinette rectangles the size of the area you want to shade, using the same number of rows and stitches in each rectangle as in the final garment section. Then when you apply the dye, paint a wider band of

unravel the swatch to learn how much of each color yarn was used. Since the number of stitches knitted in each color will vary from pattern to pattern, the proportion can vary considerably.

After unraveling the swatch into one ball or cone of main yarn and one of contrast yarn, reknit into two stockinette swatches the same number of stitches as the gauge swatch. Write down the row count for each swatch. For example, when I unraveled and reknitted one of my 48-row patterned gauge swatches, I found that the main color yielded 40 rows in stockinette, while the contrast color resulted in 31 rows. Also, measure and note your gauge for plain stockinette.

Determine how many square inches

Strong contrast, like yellow-to-orange with purple-to-blue, makes colors really sing.

silk yarn from Crystal Palace (Straw into Gold, 3006 San Pablo Avenue, Berkeley, CA 94702; 510-548-5243).

Choose a dye that's easy to use—To keep the process simple, I use Jacquard Silk basic dyes (Dharma Trading Co., PO Box 150916, San Rafael, CA 94915; 800-542-5227), which work beautifully on silk yarn. (They produce lighter colors on wool.) Available in liquid form for easy mixing, these dyes can be diluted with water for lighter shades. A free color card illustrates the 20 premixed colors and 24 blended colors (with formulas) and is a helpful reference during painting. You set the dye, or make it permanent, by immersing it in a chemical fixative solution called Dyeset or by steaming the painted fabric in a steamer. (Dharma has free instructions for making a steamer.)

If you'd like to experiment with other dyes, look for those designed for hand painting, including Pebeo Orient Express, DuPont, and Super Tinfix. Some require

the color that will be knitted last. Since you won't be using all the yarn in the finished section, painting extra yarn in the last color helps ensure its appearance in the patterned section. Save any leftover yarn for future projects.

If you're painting an entire garment, you'll want to calculate the yarn amounts more accurately. Reuse the patterned gauge swatch you knitted to chart your garment's stitches and rows. (For some tips on making a gauge swatch, see *Threads* No. 51, pp. 59-61.) Once you write down the gauge information,

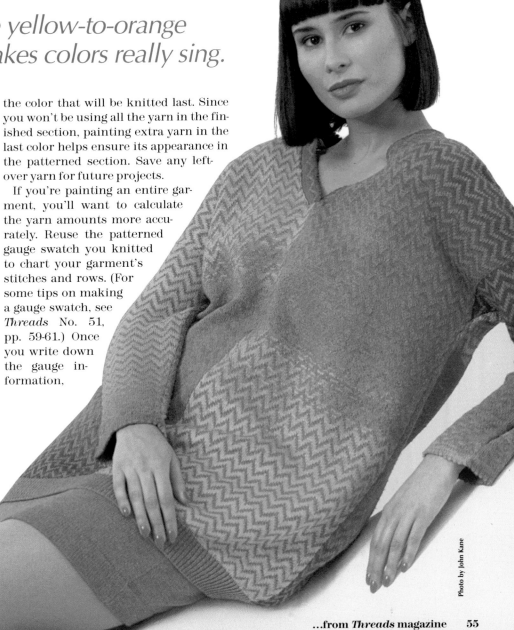

Colors can blend evenly from one end of a garment to the other when you paint the knit with permanent dye. To create shading in both yarns of a two-color pattern, you paint two separate pieces of fabric, then unravel them and reknit into one piece.

Dyeing equipment needed is simple—plastic or glass dye containers, sponge applicators, rubber gloves for safety, and a pan of water nearby for diluting colors and rinsing.

Apply the color in bands, adding water for a lighter shade and overlapping colors for a gradual transition.

you'll need for each garment section, and write them down. (For example, an 8- by 10-in. section of knitting = 80 sq. in.)

Next, divide the number of rows you knitted in stockinette for the main yarn by the number of rows in the patterned swatch. (For example, 40 rows of stockinette ÷ 48 rows of pattern = .83.) Multiply the number of square inches in the garment section by this ratio to learn the number of square inches to knit in the section you'll paint for the main yarn. (For example, 80 sq. in. x .83 = 66 sq. in.)

Finally, divide the resulting number of square inches by the width of the finished garment piece to learn how many inches to knit in length. (For example, 66 sq. in. ÷ 8-in. width = 8.25-in. length.)

Multiply the width and length measurements by the stitches and rows of the stockinette gauge to learn how many stitches and rows to knit for the main color section for that garment piece, to prepare for dyeing. (For example, 8-in. width x 4.5 st./in. = 36 st., and 8.25-in. long x 5 rows/in. = 41.25 rows; round up to 42.) Cast off loosely for easy unraveling.

That's it. Repeat the steps above to determine the size of the section to knit for the contrast yarn. Then repeat for each garment section that will contain the same Fair Isle pattern in shaded colors.

Techniques for painting with dyes

Once you've knitted the sections of natural silk, you're ready to set up a table for dyeing (see the photo above). Work in a well-ventilated area away from the kitchen, since dye chemicals aren't safe for consumption. It's best to use glass or plastic tools and containers, and reserve them exclusively for dyeing.

Some yarns contain lubricants, dirt, or oil that can interfere with the dyes. I suggest prewashing the sections by hand with Synthrapol SP (available from your dye supplier) or a solution of ¼ cup baking soda to a sinkful of hot water. Or simply wet the yarn by soaking the sections in cold water for 15 to 20 minutes; painting on wet yarn helps pull the dye into the center of the strand. Too much water will dilute the dye, however, so spin the sections in a washing machine for a couple of minutes, then store them in a plastic bag until you need them.

Now you're ready to begin the dye process. Lay the damp sections flat on plastic, as shown in the photo above, with your pencil-shaded paper pattern nearby, and begin to paint the first strip of color with a sponge applicator. You can use the dyes straight, mix colors together, or add water for lighter shades. Apply the color quickly, since once dark areas settle, the color can be difficult to remove.

To create a transition to the next color strip, add cool water and overlap the colors to blend. If the dye isn't penetrating to the wrong side, turn the fabric over and paint the reverse side also, to eliminate any pale, undyed areas.

I paint one color at a time, working from deepest saturation to lightest, then begin the next color. Or you can shade one color from dark to light over a section, as I did on the blue swatch, by adding more water with each application. The colors will lighten as they dry,

so aim darker than your desired result.

When the fabric gets too wet, roll it up from side to side so like colors are touching, and squeeze out the excess paint and water, starting at the darker end. Squeezing out the liquid further blends the colors. Don't hold the fabric with light colors below dark ones, as the darker colors will migrate. If an area gets too dark, dip the fabric into the pan of clean water to soften and blend the shades, then squeeze it out before continuing to paint.

When dyeing is complete, hang the sections to dry for at least 24 hours, away from direct sunlight; I string a clothesline indoors with plastic underneath to catch the drips. If you lay sections flat to dry, you'll get less migration of color, but drying will take longer. I actually like the "mistakes" caused by small amounts of color run-off at the sides of the sections. When reknit, these areas create an occasional ikat effect where colors change, adding texture to the finished piece.

Before unraveling and reknitting, you'll need to fix the color. With Jacquard dyes, you can soak the fabric in a mixture of fixative and water for five minutes, then rinse until the water runs clear. Although the manufacturer suggests rinsing with soap and water, in my experience, soap causes the fabric to become sticky, so I omit the soap and rinse with plain water. Or you can steam the fabric, a more involved process, for more vibrant color. After fixing, allow the panel to dry again, and you're ready for the fun part—unraveling and knitting the final garment, and seeing those beautiful colors side by side.

Of course, the obvious notion that I've left out of this story is that you don't *have* to knit in a patterned or Fair Isle design. If you want, you can simply knit one or more sections for a garment and paint on

I paint one color at a time, working from deepest saturation to lightest, then begin the next color.

gradient color for an overall effect, without ripping and reknitting. However you choose to use this painting/knitting technique, if you're a color connoisseur like me, you'll thrill at the rewarding results and the fun along the way.

Rebekah Younger of Oakland, CA, is an exhibiting painter and textile artist. Her one-of-a-kind garments sell in galleries nationwide. For more information on her work and shows, call (510) 532-09214.

Start with Shaded Yarn

You don't have to knit an entire garment with this color-shading technique. It's quick and easy to try out first in a small area of a garment, such as the front panel shown at right. You can simply sew a shaded panel to the front of a solid-color sweater or inset the panel into a sweater you're knitting using one of the following methods.

• **To knit by machine:** When knitting by machine, I like to knit the separate Fair Isle panel first, leaving open stitches at the beginning and end of the panel. Knit the body of the sweater up to the point where the panel begins, and scrap off the stitches to be replaced by the panel. Then knit the shorter sections on either side of the panel one at a time, with the opposite side on hold. You can join the panel sides to the body as you knit by hanging the end stitch of every other row of the panel onto the end needle of the main body every other row. Or you can crochet or sew up the sides later, using the mattress stitch (see *Threads* No. 59, pp. 18-20). After knitting both sides, hang the top of the panel on the center needles and continue knitting the front. Later, attach the lower edge of the panel to the body by hand, using the Kitchener stitch for an invisible seam.

• **To knit by hand:** You have a variety of options for knitting an inset into a garment. You can either knit the panel first following the sequence described above, as a machine knitter would; knit the front all at once using traditional intarsia; or try the new technique for knitting intarsia one section at a time, as discussed in the article on pp. 58-61. —*R.Y.*

Start by painting and knitting a small inset in gradient color. Then incorporate it into a sweater in progress, or simply sew it onto a plain sweater. The graphed chart above right shows how to work out the color, shading, and design first in pencil.

Photo by Yvonne Taylor

Knit In Blocks of Color— without Bobbins

Adding color, one block at a time, takes the headache out of intarsia knitting

by Rick Mondragon

Simplify knitting a complex color design by working it block by block. *With this approach, you can knit just one or two colors at a time and join the units at the edges so they look just like traditional intarsia.*

*g*arments with blocks of color knitted in are intriguing to look at and wear, but they can be daunting to make. Intarsia, also known as color or block or tapestry knitting, often uses many colors across a single row. The process can involve a maddening tangle of separate bobbins for each color hanging at the back of the work and the agonizing ripping out of rows, stitch by stitch, to make design changes or repair mistakes.

I've developed an unusual solution to these problems: Knitting one block of color at a time and building the fabric shape by shape, rather than one entire row at a time, eliminates the need for bobbins. You join one area to the next as you knit with a simple locking technique. You don't need any tools other than knitting needles and probably a crochet hook in the beginning.

To use this technique, plan your intarsia design in the usual way on graph paper (see p. 61) or start with a graphed pattern. Then decide on the knitting path, or order in which to knit the color sections. While knitting, if you don't like a color or need to correct a mistake, you only have to rip out that one section. As a result, you'll find intarsia knitting less frustrating and more enjoyable.

A loop locks the edges

When the knitting is complete, my new intarsia looks just like traditional intarsia, with the edge stitches of adjacent sections locked together. But instead of joining the edges the traditional way by wrapping the yarns as you change colors across a row, you create these wraps as each block is knitted.

Joining the edges is done as you knit the new block by pulling a loop of the working yarn through the back of an edge stitch of the finished block, as shown in the drawing on p. 60. This loop becomes what I call a *sliding loop*, since you slide more yarn into the loop through the edge stitch as needed, first knitting one row away from the edge, then a second row back towards it. When two rows are complete, you tighten the yarn loop to remove the slack, pull a new loop through the edge stitch two rows up, and repeat the process. (Note that you'll gain more speed and find it easier to follow a graph if you learn how to knit backwards—see *Threads* No. 57, p. 20—which allows you to work every row from the right side without turning the work after each row.)

The back of the edge stitch that you pull the sliding loop through is what I call the

turning thread, because it connects the last stitch in a row to the first stitch in the next row. It occurs at alternate edges of the knitting and can be difficult to locate at first, because the edge stitches tend to curl and distort. Tugging a lower edge stitch downward, as shown in the center drawing on p. 60, smooths the edge and makes the turning thread easier to see. When you hook the turning thread and pull it to the side, the edge stitches should look normal and fully formed.

When knitting a section, don't knit a special selvage edge, such as a slip-stitch or garter-stitch selvage. Every stitch will show in the finished fabric, just as it does in traditional intarsia, so the edges should be knitted in the same stitch pattern as the block.

The knitting path is key

Since each block builds on the block before, it's important to map out the knitting path. You can work each garment section from right to left, from left to right, or from the center block out on both sides. But once you determine which path is most logical to build a design, you need to stick with it throughout the section. You can't, for example, knit a block between two existing blocks unless you cut the working yarn and pull the end through the turning thread on alternating sides. This technique is a hassle and should be reserved for repairs and dire emergencies.

The flow chart below shows a logical

path for one piece of knitting. This is just an example; experiment to determine the best path for your design.

Straight-sided blocks are easiest

Since vertical stripes or blocks with straight sides are the easiest to knit block by block, let's look at these shapes first. For an example, see the photo on p. 60. After you decide on the knitting order and knit the first block (then place its stitches on a holder), join and knit the second block to the first. Depending on what direction you're working, you can add the second block to the right or left side of the first. To cast on stitches for new blocks, use the long-tail or half-hitch cast-on (see *Threads* No. 54, p. 20), which requires two strands; then purl the first row.

You can add from the right—To add a new section at the right edge of a block, you first have to cast on. Use the knitting needle or a crochet hook to pull a loop through the first cast-on knot of the existing block, as shown in the top drawing on p. 60. Pull the loop to lengthen it, make a slip knot at the right end of the loop, then use the two strands of the loop to cast on toward the existing block until you reach the number of stitches needed.

To continue knitting, remove the extra slack from the thread and pull a loop through the next turning thread, two rows up. Open the loop and use it to knit two rows, across and back. Again, remove the extra slack and repeat. ⇨

A FLOW CHART SHOWS LOGICAL KNITTING ORDER

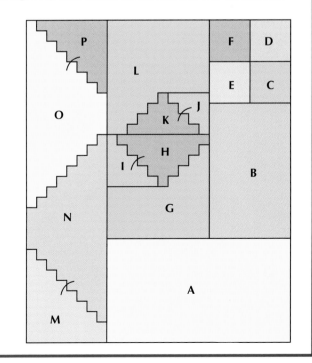

You can work from right to left, left to right, or from the center block out, but once you plan the order, follow it throughout. In this example, the knitting order flows alphabetically from right to left and bottom to top.

When necessary, work two sections together as a unit. Notice the diamond between G and L: To avoid knitting a narrow-to-wide shape that can't stand alone, such as H or J, work together as a unit with adjacent section—for example, H and I together, J and K together.

⌒ indicates units

STRAIGHT-SIDED BLOCKS ARE EASIEST

Instead of knitting with many colors across a full row, it's simpler to knit one entire section of color at a time.

To lock edges of adjacent blocks: *With crochet hook or tip of knitting needle, pull loop of new yarn through turning thread at back of edge stitch. Pull loop open and use it to knit two rows, a and b. Remove slack, then pull loop through next turning thread, two rows up, and repeat.*

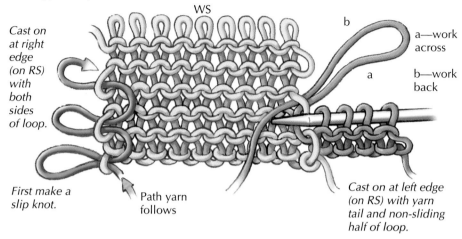

Cast on at right edge (on RS) with both sides of loop.

First make a slip knot.

Path yarn follows

WS

b

a—work across

b—work back

a

Cast on at left edge (on RS) with yarn tail and non-sliding half of loop.

Where *is* the turning thread?

Since knitted edges tend to curl, it can be tricky to locate the turning thread, where the thread from the end of one row turns to begin the next row.

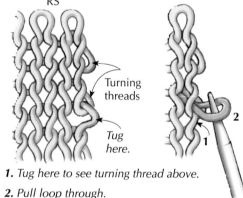

RS

Turning threads

Tug here.

1. *Tug here to see turning thread above.*

2. *Pull loop through.*

ANGLED BLOCKS ARE BUILT THE SAME WAY

Form slopes using short rows, with slipped stitches at edges held on needle until ready to work with adjacent color.

W1 = work 1 from first block

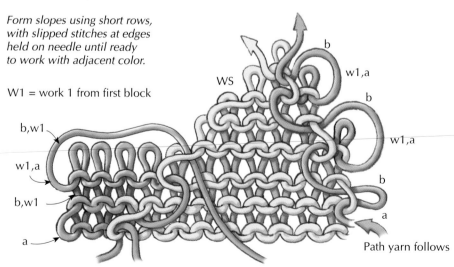

b,w1

w1,a

b,w1

a

WS

w1,a

b

b

w1,a

b

a

Path yarn follows

Where possible, knit mountains (shapes that go from wide to narrow—tan triangle) first; then join cliffs (shapes that go from narrow to wide—blue section) to them.

Or you can add from the left—To add a new section at the left side of a block, you'll start one row higher. Use the needle tip or crochet hook to pull a loop through the turning thread between rows 1 and 2 (see the top drawing at left). Open the loop, leaving a long tail. Cast on with the long tail and the first half of the loop, and purl back with the second half.

Continue knitting as before by removing extra slack and pulling a new loop through the next turning thread two rows up.

A few tips for even edges—To get smooth, even block edges that look like traditional intarsia, maintain even tension, especially at the beginning and end of the joining loops. If necessary after the knitting is complete, run a knitting needle in and out of the edges of a block and tug to smooth and adjust the tension.

Now try other shapes

After you're comfortable with knitting one vertical block at a time, you can try knitting other shapes, such as triangles or random forms. To knit a curve or an angle, don't use decreases or increases, since they don't occur in traditional intarsia and will not look right. Instead shape a block using short rows, or partially knitted rows with slipped stitches at the ends (see *Threads* No. 56, p. 22). But unlike ordinary short rows, you don't have to wrap at the end of the row to prevent a hole—pulling the loop through the edge stitch to knit the next block will accomplish the same result.

Straight-sided shapes are easiest for learning block-by-block knitting. You can mix colors, textures, and yarns to get an interesting effect within simple stripes, squares, and rectangles.

Where's the turning thread on an angle?—Joining shapes with angled sides follows the same principles as joining straight blocks, but it's a bit more complicated. In addition to pulling a loop through the turning thread, you also knit the open stitches that occur along the angles (see the bottom drawing at left). You'll knit the open stitches at the beginning or end of a row, depend-

Illustration by Clarke Barre

ing on which row they occur in. And whether you knit an open stitch every row or not will depend on how quickly you decreased on the original block.

Locating the turning thread is also trickier on angles, because of the open stitches. When there's an open stitch at the edge, I find that the easiest way to locate the turning thread is to slip the first two stitches to the left-hand needle, pick up the turning thread (it will be the uppermost thread leading to the right-hand needle), and then return the second stitch to the right-hand needle. When you begin the next row with the new loop, the first stitch to knit will be the slipped stitch.

Knitting angles in order—When knitting angles, you have to knit the lower sections first, then the neighboring shapes that hang over them. This rule about angles is illustrated on the facing page: Knit mountains (shapes that start wide and become narrower) first, then knit cliffs (shapes that start narrower and then widen) onto them. You can't knit a cliff, or narrow-to-wide shape, on its own, because you won't have a place to attach the new stitches you add as you widen the shape.

Knit two sections as a unit

This is one situation where my technique needs to be combined with traditional intarsia, so that you work just two sections together across a row. When you're working across the chart, say, from right to left, and the next block you need to knit is a narrow-to-wide cliff shape, you can't knit this shape by itself; you'll have to knit the section together with the one next to it using traditional intarsia, which I call *knitting a unit.* You carry both yarns at the back of the work and twist them together between colors (for more on traditional intarsia, see *Threads* No. 56, pp. 20, 22).

A good example of knitting in units occurs with the diamond shape shown in the flow chart on p. 59: You can knit section G (which is a mountain) by itself, but then you'll have to knit section H together with some other section. You'll knit sections H and I together as a unit, then knit J and K together as the next unit, followed by L.

You can use the same principles to knit other shapes, such as circles, small motifs, and narrow lines. Curves are treated the same way as angles, and circles and dots the same way as diamonds. Analyze your graph to determine which pairs of blocks to work in units and which blocks to work alone.

From a Painting to a Sweater

I love to turn strong visual images into garments. The sweater on p. 58 evolved from a contemporary painting by Helen Hardin. Flipping through a magazine, I stopped short at the image and knew that I wanted to knit it.

To convert a photo or other image into a knittable chart, the first step is to transfer the design lines to graph paper. Even though knit stitches are rectangular, I prefer to use standard 10 squares/in. graph paper, as shown below. To prevent the shapes from becoming distorted short and wide, I add rows while knitting by duplicating every fifth or sixth row, or combining parts of both.

I didn't want to copy the painting exactly but rather to interpret its parts in my own way. Even after charting a design, I don't use it as an exact road map, but as a guide from which I occasionally stray. The sweater front most closely echoes the original art, while the back repeats the major shapes but with fewer details. For the sleeves, I borrowed elements of the design and arranged them to unify the sweater. For example, the checks at the top of the right shoulder are repeated in both sleeves for balance.

Using my new intarsia technique, it was easy to knit the design with one or two colors at a time. Imagine the mess if I'd had to knit straight across each row! In particular, I find it easier to work tiny motifs and narrow lines in units with an adjacent block. —*R.M.*

Plot a color diagram on graph paper to translate a design into a map for knitting. Next, plan the knitting path, or order of blocks to knit, before you begin the actual knitting.

Try it for other knitting, too

I hope you'll find this technique as freeing for you as it has been for the knitters I've taught. You can use the same method to break other types of knitting into manageable chunks. Try it for cables, gansey yokes, aran stripes or blocks, or knit/purl sampler-style work. For a ruched or seersucker effect, try knitting fingering-weight yarn on size 3 needles next to mohair on size 10 needles. Once you get the hang of it, you can work all kinds of complicated knitting, one block at a time. □

Rick Mondragon of Albuquerque, NM, teaches knitting workshops across the country. He recently completed a 7-ft. 3-in. knitted portrait of Cher.

Light and Lustrous Bouclé

The textures and colors of this three-plied yarn make even the simplest sweater special

by Linda Welker

Knitting mohair bouclé for the first time was an exciting experience for me. The soft yarn made a fabric that was light, springy, thick, and incredibly textured, and it felt wonderful. Since that first swatch, I've designed and knit many garments with these special yarns.

In addition to being a knitter, I'm also a spinner, so I've been exploring texture and color by making my own bouclés. Much of what I've learned about bouclé can be applied by knitters who buy commercially available yarns (see *Fall Yarn Review, Threads* No. 54, p. 82).

If you've never had the pleasure of working with bouclé, let me show you what it offers for texture, color, and garment details. You may find it hard to go back to "plain" yarns.

Bouclé structure

To take advantage of bouclé's unique characteristics in your knitting, it helps to become familiar with its fiber composition and twist. The term *bouclé* can refer to many different-looking yarns (see the samples on the facing page for examples), but each is made similarly. A bouclé is made of three separate strands: one strand forms the soft loops, and two finer strands, called *binders*, hold the yarn together. Each strand is called a *single*. Bouclé gets its integrity from the way each strand and the yarn as a whole is spun and plied.

When I'm making a bouclé, I start by spinning the separate strands (loop—A, and binder strands—B and C) all with a Z-twist (for a description of twist, see *Threads* No. 54, p. 20). The second binder, C, has some extra twist. The finer the three strands are, the lighter the final knit fabric will be.

The strands are plied in two steps: First I spin loop strand A loosely with binder B, using a Z-twist. To do this, I hold binder B firmly in my left hand, feeding from straight in front of me into the spindle of the spinning wheel. I hold loop yarn A more loosely in my right hand, at an angle to my right. With the wheel turning slowly, I ply the two strands, manipulating the tension of strand A so that it spirals into loops loosely around B. To finish, I ply AB with C, using an S-twist, holding the binder and AB with equal tension. Strand C locks the loops into place.

As a result of their composition, when bouclés are knitted, they form soft, thick fabrics that are surprisingly lightweight, with great body and drape.

Loop fibers—Almost any soft fiber, including mohair, wool, silk, or synthetics, can be used for the loopy strand of bouclé. I am fond of mohair because it has a light, airy quality. Kid mohair, from the first two clippings of a young angora goat, is the finest and softest mohair, and it knits into soft, drapey fabric. Heavier yearling mohair, from the third clip, is still wonderful and has a lot of body. It makes a bit heavier fabric with a more dramatic "halo," as loops spread and get slightly fuzzy when worn. Even fine adult mohair, from the fourth clip on, is a lustrous and acceptable fiber for bouclé. Most commercial mohair bouclés contain yearling and fine adult mohair.

Mohair is only one of the fibers spun as the loop strand in a bouclé. Silk and wool/silk or mohair/silk blends yield a heavier yarn, with less fuzziness and luster than mohair.

Wool bouclé has a matte surface and it can make a springier, firmer fabric than mohair. Silk bouclé made from the long cocoon filaments can be lustrous, with a soft drape when knitted. Other silks, like tussah, from a wild silkworm, and noil, made from short silk fibers, have a matte surface and can have an almost crunchy feel.

Binder characteristics—The binder threads, which determine a bouclé's springiness and elasticity, can also be made from various fibers. For yarn with good recovery from being stretched, I usually spin a crimpy wool, such as that from Corriedale or Columbia sheep. This will result in a fabric that will maintain its shape. Silk, when used as a binder thread, adds a lustrous touch to fine kid mohair, but it must be spun a bit more tightly than wool for elasticity.

Many commercial bouclés have some nylon in the binder for durability, but too much nylon can make the bouclé scratchy.

Shape of the loop—The texture of a fabric knit from bouclé varies with the density, distribution, and nature of the loops along the yarn. ⇨

Bouclé loops determine a knit fabric's character: Two fine threads wrap around a loose one to create loops. The fine threads can be a fiber, like wool, or a metallic.

From *Threads* magazine (August 1994) 54:42-45

Basic stitch, simple shape: Stockinette turned purl side out displays bouclé to its best advantage as shown in this jacket made of handspun kid mohair and wool. The fabric's structure needs no special finishing, no facings, and no ribbings.

Photo by Susan Kahn

A simple pattern for a bouclé jacket

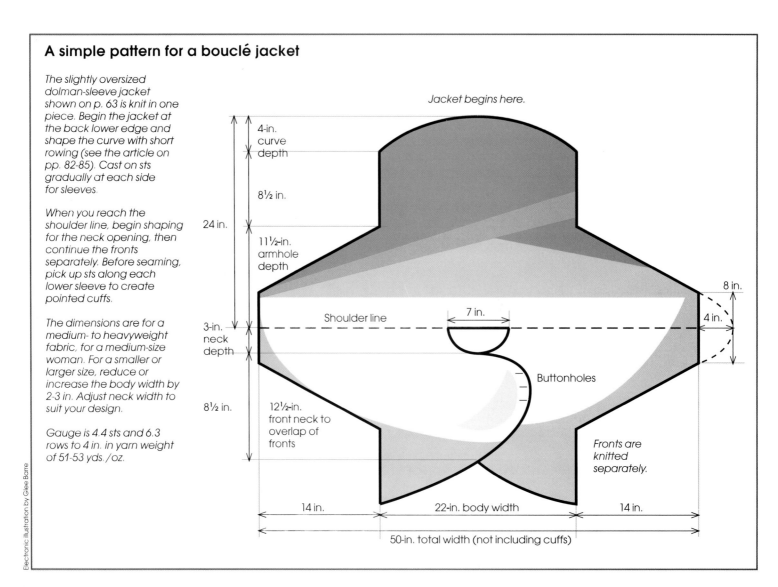

The slightly oversized dolman-sleeve jacket shown on p. 63 is knit in one piece. Begin the jacket at the back lower edge and shape the curve with short rowing (see the article on pp. 82-85). Cast on sts gradually at each side for sleeves.

When you reach the shoulder line, begin shaping for the neck opening, then continue the fronts separately. Before seaming, pick up sts along each lower sleeve to create pointed cuffs.

The dimensions are for a medium- to heavyweight fabric, for a medium-size woman. For a smaller or larger size, reduce or increase the body width by 2-3 in. Adjust neck width to suit your design.

Gauge is 4.4 sts and 6.3 rows to 4 in. in yarn weight of 51-53 yds./oz.

Electronic illustration by Glee Barre

Jacket begins here.

4-in. curve depth

8½ in.

24 in.

11½-in. armhole depth

3-in. neck depth

8½ in.

Shoulder line

7 in.

8 in.

4 in.

Buttonholes

12½-in. front neck to overlap of fronts

Fronts are knitted separately.

14 in.

22-in. body width

14 in.

50-in. total width (not including cuffs)

The more tightly packed the loops are along the yarn, the thicker the fabric will be. Bouclés with closely placed loops or those with poor elasticity produce fabrics that tend to grow with wear. Use these thick yarns for accessories or as accents.

Bouclés with evenly spaced loops will knit into relatively smooth fabrics, in which color and detailing are shown to their best advantage.

For a fabric with textural variations, I spin bouclé so the loop strand is distributed unevenly with the first binder, with some areas more tightly twisted than others. When plied with the second binder, the highly twisted areas form gnarls and corkscrews. You can also buy bouclés with this character. Commercial bouclés can have slubs or extended corkscrews where the soft strand twists rather than curls. This creates irregular loops, for a more jazzy and complex yarn and fabric.

Keep the stitch pattern simple

Because bouclé makes such a rich fabric, it's best used with the simplest of stitch patterns—basic stockinette. A bouclé tex-ture hides all but the simplest knitting stitches, and even the structure of stockinette stitches disappear. Because the purl side of stockinette has a more horizontal alignment of yarn, it tends to be more textured. When you knit with bouclé, most of the curls, and the texture, appear on the purl side. The knit side, where stitches are vertically aligned, has a flatter surface, and the color of the binder threads is highlighted.

Swatching

The best way to get acquainted with bouclé yarns is to knit swatches with them. Knit large swatches, at least 8 in. square. Pin them up to hang, unweighted, for a week. This will give you a sense of the final gauge, drape, and elasticity of the fabric.

I suggest you try several needle sizes to find a fabric that you like best. To start, look at your bouclé strand. If the loops are spaced fairly far apart, then yarn weight is more closely related to the thickness of the binder threads, and the yarn will look better if knit with smaller needles. When the loops are packed close together, they contribute more weight to the strand, so use larger needles.

You can tell a great deal about the fabric by handling the swatch itself. Stretch it from side to side, and from top to bottom. If it springs back nicely and holds its shape, you've probably chosen a good needle size. If it is loose or lacking body, try a smaller needle. If it seems too dense, try a slightly larger needle.

Working with bouclé

Knitting bouclé can feel clumsy at first, as you might knit into a loop or a binder rather than into the complete stitch. Think of the yarn as a unit as you work and you'll be less likely to knit into one of its parts. Weave ends as you go, twisting them with the working strand so they completely disappear into the fabric.

Cast on and bind off loosely and carefully with bouclé. I like the long-tail method of casting on, but you can use any cast-on that will create an elastic edge. Picking up stitches and increasing and decreasing are more difficult with this bulky, sometimes slippery yarn. If you must rip out, do it carefully, stitch by stitch, to avoid ruining a length of yarn.

To ensure that the lower edges of a sweater lie flat, I knit the first 1 to 2 in. of every piece in garter stitch (knit every row). If your garter-stitch gauge is not the same as stockinette, use a smaller needle at the edges. I also knit five stitches at side edges in garter stitch for firmness. To join pieces, choose a smooth, strong yarn and use whatever seaming method would create the least bulk at a seam. It works best to catch only half a stitch from each edge.

Color

Most of the color of bouclé fabric is determined by the loops of the yarn, but binder threads, although fine, contribute color as well. For subtle coloration, look for bouclés with binder colors that match the loop color. For a little contrast, use a bouclé that has binders that are lighter or darker than the loop. This yields a fabric

> *Bouclé makes such a rich fabric that it's best knit with basic stockinette.*

with a tweedy effect that will be apparent when the garment is worn. For a hint of glitter, use a bouclé that has a metallic thread as one binder.

My favorite way to use color within a garment is to choose similar colors for subtle transitions. For instance, you might choose several shades of blue and green. For an even subtler blend, the blues and greens should be of the same value (same lightness or darkness). For a bit more contrast, try mixing medium and dark blues with medium and dark greens.

To add an enlivening accent to closely related color groups, add one or two very different colors. For example, to green/blue combinations, you could add a rosy pink accent. An occasional thin line, or even just a few stitches, will enliven without overwhelming the blended effect of your main color scheme.

A neutral color knitted between strong colors can act as shading or crosshatching. For instance, I often use silver or gray as a neutral between cool colors such as green and blue. With warmer, earthier colors, like rusts, oranges, and

browns, you might use beiges or taupes.

When you're planning a bouclé garment, here's a tip to use while deciding on colors: Mohair bouclé skeins tend to resemble the knit fabric, so I've found that I can lay skeins side by side to mock up the areas of color in the final fabric.

Garment possibilities

A simple shape is often all that is needed when working with bouclé. (Keeping the structure basic frees you to explore color and shaping at cuffs and hems.) I use a kimono shape—basically square, with overlapping fronts—as a basis for most of my designs. I manipulate this shape, then think about details like cuffs and collars to further enhance the design. You can use a simple knitting pattern or a sewing pattern as a guide. Or, measure a garment that is made from a yarn of the same weight as your bouclé and that fits well, and use the measurements to plan your garment. If you don't have anything appropriate, you can scale up the jacket schematic on the facing page.

Since bouclé yarns have a lot of body, edges maintain their shape. You don't need ribbings or separate button bands; buttonholes can be knit right into the garter or stockinette edge. Knitted bouclé fabrics also lend themselves to nontraditional shaping. You can work unusually shaped edges, with curves or points.

One of the great things about bouclé is that you can go back and add to areas of your garment even after the pieces are done, and the pick-up won't show. On my jacket, for example, I changed the shape of the underlap of the front (which was knitted with a straight edge) after the garment was completed by picking up stitches, knitting a few rows, and binding off gradually to create a curve.

Closures require special attention. I work buttonholes by binding off one or two stitches, then casting on the same number of stitches above the bound-off ones. To reinforce buttonholes, I blanket-stitch around the openings. (See the detail photo at right). To support the weight of the buttons, I knit 1-in. square pads and sew them to the wrong side of the fabric before sewing on the buttons.

At last

I've enjoyed my explorations of these wonderful yarns, and I've knit many successful designs with them. I encourage you to use bouclés to create a colorful, textured garment of your own. □

Fiber artist Linda Welker is currently weaving and is working on a series of fiber collages at her Forest Grove, OR, studio.

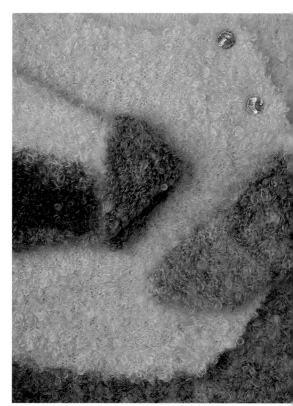

Lots of texture hides seams: *When you pick up along any edge of a bouclé fabric, the join is barely visible because of the deep texture. You can add shaped details, such as a cuff (shown here) or even a curved lower edge, after a garment is complete.*

Buttonholes are simple: *Cast stitches off and on in bouclé to create an opening. Then blanket stitch (shown from the right side, top, and wrong side, bottom) around the opening for additional firmness.*

Designing with Spring and Summer Yarns

Challenging fibers reward knitters with fabulous color and texture

by Deborah Newton

*a*s a freelance knitwear designer, I've had experience with dozens of warm-weather yarns. They are definitely more challenging than those yarns and fibers we associate with the winter season, but I do like them for their unique qualities. To design effectively with them, I've learned to exercise a few precautions. I've also stopped comparing them to my favorite fiber, wool, and now expect different things of them.

Although you can use some winter yarns like lightweight wool and mohair for cool summer-weather garments, especially in openwork patterns; the yarns traditionally offered for spring and summer are usually made from cotton, linen, rayon, and blends. These natural and man-made fibers tend to be a bit heavy and to lack elasticity. But I am always thrilled with the bright, clear color range that the cotton yarns offer. Mercerized cottons and most rayons have a bright sheen or at least a soft glow. I also like the dusty, matte look of many of the pastel linen blends. There is also a wide range of textures, from subtle cabled twists to bold yarns with large wormlike slubs.

Design considerations

A designer's job is to use a yarn to its best advantage, so I try to identify what makes each yarn unique and enhance its good qualities. For example, if a yarn has intriguing texture, I look for a way to emphasize this feature, as I did with "Irish Linen," shown in the bottom photo on p. 71. If it is smooth and plain, I know that bold color or interesting pattern will become the focus.

You can't avoid the fact that many summer yarns create heavy fabrics. I try to knit them firmly so that the resulting fabric will retain its shape. When designing a large garment, I make sure that the seams, especially at the shoulders, are strong and that the join between body and edgings is never slack. With cardigans, I often knit the edging separately and sew it on for a firm join.

Ribbing tends to be less successful with summer yarns, so I often use it for accent rather than to create a close fit. If I do want a blouson effect above a ribbed edge, I weave a double strand of strong elastic thread through the last wrong-side rib row after the garment is complete. With textured yarns, ribbing can be virtually invisible and inelastic, so I usually consider another kind of flat edging, like garter stitch.

Deborah Newton's sophisticated, classic shell of rayon ribbon yarn is ideal for dressy or career wear, spring through autumn. Complete pattern instructions begin on p. 72. (Photo by Yvonne Taylor)

Finally, garments knitted with summer yarns tend not to wear as long as those knitted with wool, so I avoid intricate projects. Uncomplicated garment shapes and simple details are best suited to these less accommodating yarns. A strong, lightweight cotton is the exception, making for a truly long-wearing summer garment.

Swatching

Swatching is the best way to get acquainted with a yarn and find out what it can or can't do. When planning a design or substituting yarns, work a larger swatch than you would normally knit to measure gauge (at least 6 in. by 6 in.). Swatching will test your needle size, check the effectiveness of the pattern, and test how patterns combine. When your swatch is finished, you can drape it, stretch it, and get a feel for how the fabric will translate to a garment.

In fact, whether you are following a pattern or designing a garment with summer yarns, it's crucial to knit a good-sized swatch to obtain gauge and to check the firmness of your fabric. Two swatches, each worked with a different needle size, can often have almost the same gauge, but one will feel slightly firmer. Since fabrics knit with these yarns tend to stretch with wear, knit two swatches with different needles and choose the firmer one.

I also use swatching to explore my ideas before beginning an actual project. For example, I experiment with different pattern or color combinations. I test my finishing methods on my swatches as well. If you think that swatching is tedious or a waste of your time, I can only encourage you with my own success: Whenever I've been pleased with my swatch, I have never been disappointed with the fabric of the garment that follows.

Tips for working with summer yarns

I tend to use one needle size smaller with summer yarn than I would for a wool yarn of the same weight. If you knit loosely, you'll want to drop down two sizes. If you are unsure, swatch quickly in stockinette over 4 in. to find a desirable tension before beginning your larger swatch.

To avoid a slack fabric when working knit/purl patterns and ribbings, tug firmly when changing the yarn from front to back.

In colorwork patterns, join new colors at the edge by tying a loop in the new yarn, slipping the old yarn through the loop, and pulling the new yarn firmly up against the edge (see *Threads* No. 33, p. 22).

Use a very fine needle for the initial pickup row along edges so there is a firm join between edging and main fabric. Separately knit edging should be slightly shorter than the garment edge. Pin it in place, stretching slightly, then sew.

Weaving in ends is an eternal problem with slippery yarns. To avoid having ends that pop out, I often weave them into the seams, which tend to stretch less than the main fabric.

Developing design ideas

To give you an idea of how I deal with summer yarns, I've knit swatches in some of my favorite yarns, using them in ways that have worked for me. Each swatch inspired a special summer garment, shown in my sketches on the following pages.

I've chosen yarn types that are usually available in the spring/summer season; although some are truly unique, like the variegated rayon on p. 71, top. Solid color cottons, similar to those that I have used, are available from many different sources in almost any color imaginable. Three of my swatches use colors that pair well with traditional summer fabrics like madras, tropical prints, and batiks. I also swatched colors that work well with white and linen. Clear blues always seem right for the summer; and deep taupe, which I chose for my rayon ribbon shell, shown on the facing page, adds a touch of sophistication.

When I swatched "Glacé" from Berroco, preparatory to designing this shell (pattern on p. 72), I looked for a stitch pattern that would show off the flatness of the ribbon and allow it to drape. Slipstitch patterns are often successful since they elongate the stitches, as are patterns where the yarn is carried across the right side of the fabric. This time I tried an unusual cable look-alike that I found in an old *Mon Tricot* pattern book. The yarn is wrapped twice around the needle, with the elongated stitches extended over several rows. I used the same technique to make a textured single-stitch accent line to divide the "cables."

After slight steaming, the swatch draped beautifully, and I sketched a very simple shell with a classic-fitting silhouette that drapes slightly. The broad shoulder forms a small capped-sleeve effect, which I've enhanced by working the armhole ribbing wider over the top of the shoulder than I did at the underarm. The slightly detailed ribbing enhances the simple neckline and is fun to knit.

As you explore the wealth of wonderful summer yarns in the examples that follow and in your own work, don't expect them to behave as your autumn/winter favorites do. Use them to their best advantage by choosing enticing colors and textures, by knitting your fabrics firmly, and by finishing your garments carefully. If made well, they will last long beyond their first summer, and you'll be enjoying them even in the cool months.　　⇨

Cotton yarns

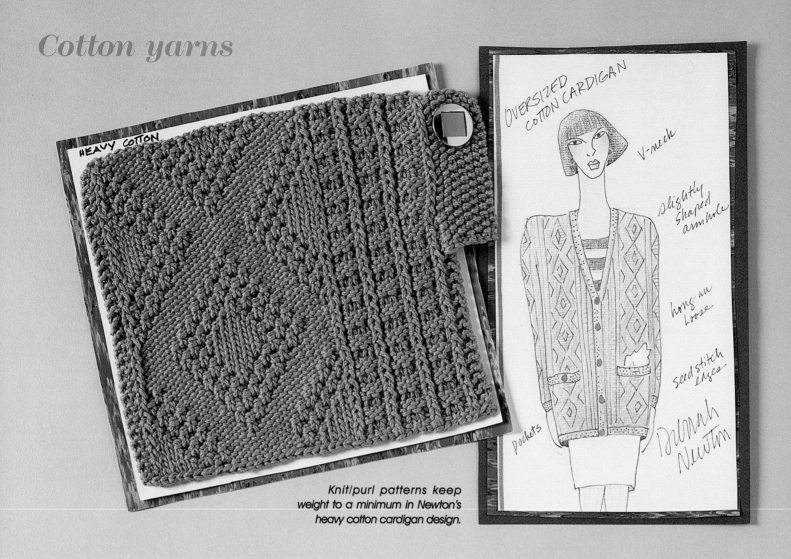

Knit/purl patterns keep weight to a minimum in Newton's heavy cotton cardigan design.

The range of 100% cotton yarns is enormous, from heavy, bulky-weight strands all the way to fine crochet cottons that look more like string than knitting yarn. In the mid-range are many wonderful worsted-weight cottons that can be worked at a gauge of 5 to 5½ sts/in. I use high-sheen yarns for colorwork and for brightening solid areas of stockinette; but for texture, I prefer cottons with a duller finish.

Heavy cotton

"Monterey," offered by Crystal Palace, is a medium-weight four-ply 100% cotton, with a suggested gauge of 4 sts/in. (70 yd./50 g ball). It has a slight sheen, with a bit of texture due to the cabled twist.

With a heavy cotton, I avoid patterns that compress the fabric and make it even heavier. A single cable works nicely as an accent, but an allover cabled pattern makes for a cumbersome garment. Colorwork also adds extra weight. Knit/purl patterns help keep the weight of the finished fabric to a minimum.

On one side of my swatch, shown above, I placed a single repeat of a diamond pattern to form a panel and flanked it with a small, blocky pattern. I found both in Barbara Walker's indispensable treasuries of knitting patterns (New York: Charles Scribner's Sons, three volumes: 1968, 1970, 1982).

I sketched a longish V-neck cardigan that could be worn open in warm weather. Because of its slightly oversized silhouette, I shaped the armhole a bit and planned a shallow sleeve cap to keep bulk to a minimum in the underarm. I used my sketch to help me plot the wide diamond panels, which I centered in the shoulder area, so the V-neckline shaping wouldn't cut into the pattern too much.

A firmly knit fabric and sewn on seedstitch edgings ensure that this cardigan will wear well. To reduce bulk, I'll make lightweight woven-fabric inner pockets, rather than knitted pocket linings.

Smooth, medium-weight cottons

This weight of cotton yarn is not overly heavy and is suitable for cables and stranded colorwork, as well as eyelet patterns and lace that is not too open. One of my favorite medium-weight cottons is mercerized "Newport Light" from Classic Elite because of its extensive color range that includes many sophisticated shades. This shiny yarn knits into a buttery soft fabric.

For my colorwork swatch at near right, facing page, I chose a warm grouping of main colors, inspired by summer vegetables—carroty orange, bell pepper green, and tomato red. For background interest, I chose some light shades that are quite different from each other: a tawny yellow, a pearly pale mauve, and a light taupe.

I wanted bold patterning to allow the many colors to keep their separate identities, so I chose a traditional Scandinavian pattern that, in this yarn and color combination, takes on a graphic quality. To add a touch of texture and to act as pattern dividers, I worked bands of twisted stitches. Another small swatch combined ribbing and a twist-stitch cable, a detail inspired by the textured bands in the body. I tipped the ribbing with one of the colors for detail.

Since so much was happening in the fabric, I chose a simple shape and silhouette, an oversized pullover, again with a little armhole shaping. After

Medium-weight cottons are suitable for color work. Newton adds a textured stitch divider for additional interest.

Fine cottons require a substantial investment of time, but they are ideal for classic garments that will remain fashionable, like this blue lace top.

SMOOTH MEDIUM WEIGHT COTTON

FINE GAUGE COTTON

LIGHT WEIGHT COTTON SHORT SLEEVE PULLOVER

crisp lace

tiny-rolled edges

Delmah Newton

OVERSIZED PULLOVER

wide slit at neckline

slight armhole shaping

twist stitch accent

ribbing tipped in orange

blended background colors

bright vegetable main colors

shiny cotton

Delmah Newton

sketching several neckline variations, I settled on a rather wide neckline, framed with a wide ribbing to add interest to the simple shape. Experience has taught me that this kind of neckline is a bit tricky, requiring gradual decreases in the shoulder area to lie flat. Otherwise, the collar will stand up slightly.

Fine-gauge cotton
The many choices include mercerized, tightly plied, softly twisted, and even crochet cottons. These are the "investment" yarns for summer—strong, long-wearing, and worth the extra time. I chose a crisp 100% cotton yarn from Rowan called "Cabled Mercerized Cotton." I was attracted by its slightly grainy texture and hard edge.

I wanted a lace with some body and selected an unusually graphic Bavarian pattern that features diagonal stripes of flat stockinette alternating with a textured, ribbed lace. My fabric, above, was firm and crisp, with excellent pattern definition. Rather than use traditional ribbing, I picked up and worked an edging of tiny reverse stockinette ridges over 10% fewer stitches than the swatch body.

The best designs for time-consuming fine-gauge fabrics are those with classic appeal that can be worn for many seasons. I sketched a simple pullover with a rather close-fitting silhouette. The armhole is shaped to bring the garment in toward the body's actual shoulder line, necessitating a full cap for the elbow-length sleeves. Although you can't see from my sketch, the lower edge is ribbed, so it can be tucked into a waistband without bulk. A small keyhole opening at the back neck closes with one button and allows the garment to pass over the head easily. ⇨

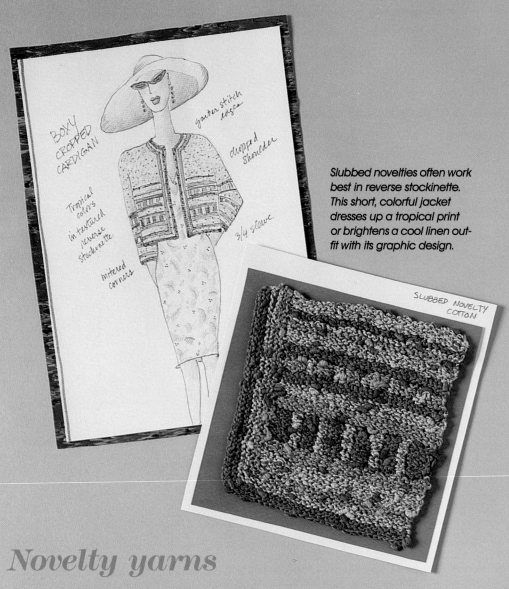

Slubbed novelties often work best in reverse stockinette. This short, colorful jacket dresses up a tropical print or brightens a cool linen outfit with its graphic design.

Novelty yarns

You can never tell what a novelty yarn will do until you swatch it, so I buy one ball when I'm considering a novelty. I choose yarns that have some body, and I avoid those that feel scratchy or slippery. Cotton and cotton blend novelties are generally reliable, particularly those with a firm twist. Fluffy, loosely spun yarns tend to fuzz and wear out fast. I only use 100% synthetic yarns for accent since they are usually difficult to work with and don't wear well.

Slubbed novelty cotton

A whimsical 100% cotton novelty, "Salsa," from Crystal Palace (95 yd./50 g ball) appealed to me. Each ball had a linen-y look, in a two-color blend, with wiry texture and good-sized slubs. Because I like a challenge, I chose three contrasting balls: A pale olive/ivory for the background, and for contrast, a hot gold/olive and a deep turquoise/royal blue. I hoped that the cool background

would make the bold colors look even brighter—but only swatching would tell.

With many textured yarns, reverse stockinette is the most successful fabric because the horizontal bars of the purl stitches push the texture forward. For my swatch, shown above, I worked a simple stripe-and-check colorwork pattern in reverse stockinette that I devised as I knitted. To form a clean break between color areas, I knit a plain stockinette row (knit on RS rows or purl on WS rows) in the new color(s). Then I could put the purl surface of the new color on the right side on the next row.

I tested a mitered edging along the lower and side edges of my swatch, marking a center stitch at the corner, and increasing one stitch on each side of it every RS row, including the bind-off row. Flat garter stitch gave the edging a little more bulk than the main fabric.

My resulting swatch was bold and colorful, perfect for matching with a tropical print, or elegant with plain

linen. I sketched a simple, boxy cardigan, with the colorwork bordering the lower edges of body and sleeves. A dropped shoulder structure emphasizes the strong, straight lines of the pattern, and three-quarter length sleeves make this little jacket more wearable in hot weather.

Variegated rayon yarn

I was attracted to a new variegated 100% rayon, "Asia" from Classic Elite, with a high yardage (230 yd./100 g hank); it had a lovely drape in the skein that I hoped would be captured in the knitting. I chose a shade called "Mother-of-pearl." The yarn had little stretch, so I was anxious to see how accommodating it would be.

I tried a couple of lace patterns, but the fabric seemed skimpy. I felt the yarn called for a pattern with body and a bit of thickness, perhaps one that had garter stitch elements, or even a crochet pattern. I have been experimenting with combining knitted and crocheted fabrics, and I felt that the sophisticated coloring of the yarn would help create a delicate fabric that would avoid the "afghan" look.

I crocheted a shell-like pattern as a border for the swatch at top, facing page. Then I picked up along the upper edge, and worked a knit/purl pattern with a slightly corrugated surface. For detail, and to pick up on the lace quality of the crocheted edge, I worked eyelet stripes edged in garter stitch ridges. I found some matching mother-of-pearl buttons, which helped me settle on a cardigan-style garment. A crocheted edging added to my swatch seemed firm enough to hold the heavy buttons without stretching out.

For my cardigan, I chose a slightly oversized silhouette to show off the drape of the knitted fabric. A raglan style is often a good choice for a summer yarn because the diagonal armhole seams help support the garment's weight in the upper body. Sketching this traditionally feminine garment reminded me that I would have to plan carefully to match the horizontal stripes in the body with those in the upper sleeve where they meet at the raglan line.

Textured cotton-and-linen blend

Henry's Attic (see "Sources," facing page) offers an interesting coned yarn called "Irish Lace," (725 yd./lb.). This natural blend is 80% ivory cotton and 20% flax-colored linen, twisted together to yield a firm rickrack-like strand.

I swatched first in stockinette stitch to get a feel for the yarn, which formed strong vertical lines and reminded me of a hard-textured chenille. The reverse side had fuller texture, like terrycloth. I wanted a little more interest than these simple patterns could give, so I swatched in a few cable patterns before settling on the one that you see at lower right. For a smooth fabric, I eliminated the purl stitches that usually flank this familiar pattern, and I also extended the "wings" of every fourth repeat to make the lines travel to the fabric's edge. These simple changes made a rather lackluster cable into something special. And in this yarn, the effect was subtle and sophisticated.

Ribbing was out of the question—it was blurred and inelastic. Instead, I tried something that had occurred to me while swatching. After working two dense garter stitch ridges, I began a simple diagonal lace pattern with yarnovers worked on every row. After an inch of lace, I worked two more firm garter ridges. Decorative and open at the center, this edging was also firm and dense at its edges.

I love a ballerina neckline in a summer sweater. This style works best with raglan shaping and needs a firm edge. The finished width should allow it to sit squarely on the shoulders or slide to one side for a more provocative off-the-shoulder look.

I chose a just slightly oversized silhouette for some drape, with sleeve length a little above the wrist to keep this hip-length sweater from looking sloppy. The diagonal lines of the traveling cables visually elongate the garment, making it well suited for slightly larger figures. □

Deborah Newton is a contributing editor of Threads. *Design photos by Susan Kahn.*

Sources

Write for your nearest local distributor.

Berroco, Inc.
See p. 72

Classic Elite
12 Perkins St.
Lowell, MA 01854
(508) 453-2837

Crystal Palace
3006 San Pablo Ave.
Berkeley, CA 94702
(415) 548-9988

Henry's Attic
5 Mercury Ave.
Monroe, NY 10950
(914) 783-3930

Rowan, distributed by Westminster Trading Corp.
5 Northern Blvd.
Amherst, NH 03031
(603) 886-5041

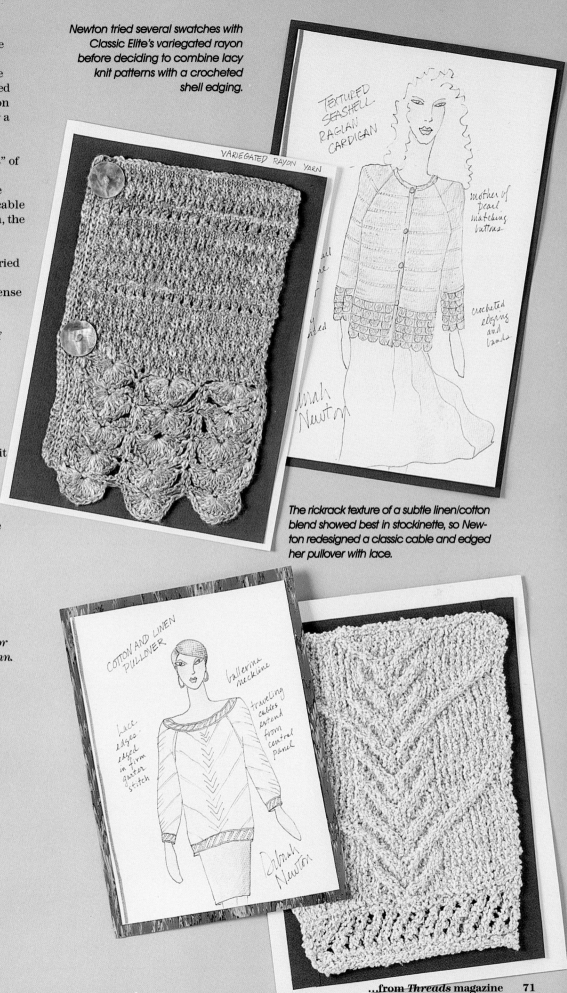

Newton tried several swatches with Classic Elite's variegated rayon before deciding to combine lacy knit patterns with a crocheted shell edging.

The rickrack texture of a subtle linen/cotton blend showed best in stockinette, so Newton redesigned a classic cable and edged her pullover with lace.

Deborah Newton's Sleeveless Ribbon Shell

This sophisticated shell features decorative slipped stitch cables on front and back, that highlight the flat rayon ribbon yarn. The fit is just loose enough to allow the fabric to drape softly. Slightly extended shoulders and short rows worked on the armhole ribbing produce a mock capped-sleeve effect.

YARN REQUIREMENTS

The shell is knit of a smooth, silky rayon ribbon that creates a fabric with a soft drape. The yarn is "Glacé" from Berroco, Inc., 100% rayon (1¾ oz. tube = 75 yd.) in color taupe #2003: 11 (12, 14, 15) tubes or approx 800 (900, 1000, 1100) yd. For your nearest supplier, contact Berroco, Inc., PO Box 367, Dept. T-3-91, Uxbridge, MA 01569; (508) 278-2527.

This ribbon yarn has unique qualities. Any substitution, even of another ribbon yarn, will yield a fabric that has a slightly different drape and texture. If you do substitute another ribbon, pick one with similar yardage, and swatch carefully to obtain the correct gauge. When working with ribbon yarn, avoid twisting the strand by allowing the tube to spin freely. You can make a spindle for this by inserting a knitting needle through a shoebox.

Needles: One pair each size 5 and 7 knitting needles, or size to obtain gauge. One 16-in. long size 5 circular knitting needle. One cable needle (cn) or double-pointed needle. One blunt tapestry needle.

Gauge: *To save time, take time to check gauge.* 20 sts and 27 rows equal 4 in. in reverse stockinette stitch with size 7 needle, slightly steamed.
Cabled panel, worked over 49 sts with a size 7 needle, should measure 7¾ in. wide, slightly steamed.

MEASUREMENTS

Directions are given for four sizes: Petite (small, medium, large), to fit 32 (34, 36, 38) in. bust. The fit should be just slightly loose, so choose a finished shell size that is approx 4 in. larger than your actual bust measurement.

STITCH DIRECTIONS

See *Threads* No. 33, p. 22, for drawings and information about the special knitting techniques employed.

Step-by-step instructions

PATTERN STITCHES

See "Key to Symbols" on facing page for abbreviations.

Ribbing: (multiple of 9 sts, plus 2). See top chart on facing page.
Row 1 (WS): k2, *(p1, k1)3x, p1, k2; rep from *.
Row 2: p2, * (k1, p1)3x, k1, p2; rep from *.
Rep rows 1 and 2.

Reverse stockinette stitch (rev st st): worked over any number of sts.
Row 1 (RS): purl.
Row 2: knit.
Rep rows 1 and 2.

Slipstitch cable pattern: (worked over a panel of 49 sts). See bottom chart on facing page.
Preparation row (RS): k1 (divider st), *p5, k2 wrapping yarn twice for each st, p1, k2 wrapping yarn twice for each st, p5, k1 (divider st); rep from * 3x.
Row 1 (WS): p1, *k5, sl 2 wyif dropping extra loops, k1, sl 2 wyif dropping extra loops, k5, p1; rep from * 3x.
Row 2: k1, *p5, sl 2 wyib, p1, sl 2 wyib, p5, k1; rep from * 3x.
Row 3: p1, *k5, sl 2 wyif, k1, sl 2 wyif, k5, p1; rep from * 3x.
Row 4: k1 wrapping yarn twice, *p3, BC4, p1, FC4, p3, k1 wrapping yarn twice; rep from * 3x.
Row 5: same as row 1, except for divider sts—sl wyif dropping extra loop.
Row 6: same as row 2, except for divider sts—sl wyib.
Row 7: same as row 3, except for divider sts—sl wyif.
Rows 8, 9, 10, 11: same as rows 4, 5, 6 and 7.
Row 12: same as row 4, except for divider sts—k.
Rep rows 1-12 only. Do not rep preparation row.

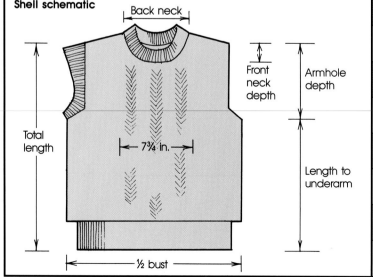

Shell schematic

Back neck · Front neck depth · Armhole depth · Total length · 7¾ in. · Length to underarm · ½ bust

Shell measurements (in inches, after seaming)				
Body (bust)	Petite (32)	Small (34)	Medium (36)	Large (38)
Finished bust at underarm	36½	38½	40½	42½
Total length (from shoulder)	22	22½	23	23½
Length to underarm (including ribbing)	14	14	14	14
Armhole depth	8	8½	9	9½
Back neck width	6½	7	7½	7¾
Front neck depth	2	2	2	2

BACK

With smaller needle, cast on 87 (96, 105, 114) sts.
Next row (WS): p2 (edge sts). Work row 1 of rib to last 2 sts, end p2 (edge sts). *Note: Work edge sts throughout in stockinette, p WS rows, k RS rows.*
Work even until rib measures 3 in.; end with a RS row.
Purl WS row, inc 16 (13, 8, 5) sts evenly spaced between edge sts at each end of row–103 (109, 113, 119) sts. Change to larger needles.

Next row (RS): k2 (cont edge sts); place marker; work in rev st st over 25 (28, 30, 33) sts; place marker; work preparation row of **Slipstitch cable** pat over center 49 sts; place marker; work in rev st st over 25 (28, 30, 33) sts; place marker; end k2 (cont edge sts).
Work even until piece measures 11 in. above rib (14 in. total); end with a WS row.

Armhole shaping: Bind off 2 sts at beg of next 8 rows–87 (93, 97, 103) sts. Keeping first and last 2 edge sts in stockinette, work even until armhole depth measures 8 (8½, 9, 9½) in.; end with a WS row.

Back neck and shoulder shaping: Bind off 8 (8, 8, 9) sts; work 25 (26, 27, 28) sts; join a second ball of yarn and bind off center 21 (25, 27, 29) sts; work to end.
Working both sides at the same time with separate balls of yarn, bind off 8 (8, 8, 9) sts at the next 3 shoulder edges; then 7 (8, 9, 9) sts at the next 2 shoulder edges.
And at the same time, bind off 5 sts from each neck edge twice.

FRONT

Work same as for back until armhole depth measures 6 (6½, 7, 7½) in., end with a WS row–87 (93, 97, 103) sts.

Front neck shaping: Next row (RS), work 38 (39, 40, 42) sts; join a second ball of yarn and bind off center 11 (15, 17, 19) sts; work rem 38 (39, 40, 42) sts to end.
Working both sides at the same time with separate balls of yarn, bind off at each neck edge 3 sts once, then 2 sts 6 times–23 (24, 25, 27) sts each side.
When armhole depth measures same as back to shoulder shaping, end with a WS row.

Shoulder shaping: From each shoulder edge, bind off 8 (8, 8, 9) sts twice and 7 (8, 9, 9) sts once.

FINISHING

Lay pieces flat. Holding warm iron an inch above surface of fabric, steam cabled and rev st st sections lightly. Do not steam ribbing. Sew front to back at shoulders and sides.

Neckline ribbing: With RS facing and circular needle, beg at right shoulder. Pick up 108 (117, 126, 126) sts evenly around entire neck edge. Place marker and join.
Next rnd: *p2, (k1, p1)3x, k1; rep from *
Rep last rnd until rib measures 1¼ in. Bind off on next rnd; *and at the same time,* p2tog in each p2 rib for first three sizes.

Left armhole ribbing: With RS facing and circular needle, beg at side seam. Pick up 44 (49, 53, 58) sts evenly along left front armhole; pick up 1 st in shoulder seam and mark this st; then pick up 45 (49, 54, 58) sts evenly along left back armhole to beg–90 (99, 108, 117) sts. Place marker and join.

Next rnd (RS): p1, *(k1, p1)3x, k1, p2; rep from *, end p1 instead of p2.
Next rnd, with four short rows: Work in rib until 12 sts have been worked on back armhole after marked st; bring yarn to front and sl next st to RHN, bring yarn to back and sl last st back to LHN to form wrap; turn. Work in rib until 12 sts have been worked on front armhole after marked st; wrap; turn. Work in rib until 21 sts have been worked on back armhole after marked st; wrap; turn. Work in rib until 21 sts have been worked on front armhole after marked st; wrap; turn. Work in rib to end of rnd. *And at the same time,* when you reach a wrapped st, work it together with the strand that wraps it.
Next rnd: rib as est; work last wrapped st tog with strand that wraps it. Work in rnds until rib at underarm measures 1 in. Bind off on next rnd, *and at the same time,* p2tog in each p2 rib, all sizes.

Right armhole ribbing: Work right armhole ribbing as for left. □

KEY TO SYMBOLS

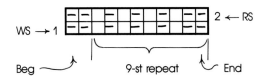

☐ *Knit (RS), purl (WS).*

– *Purl (RS), knit (WS).*

⊠ *Knit, wrapping yarn around needle twice.*

⊡ *Slip 1 purlwise wyib (RS), slip 1 purlwise wyif (WS).*

⊠⊠╱ *BC4–Slip 2 sts to cn and hold in back, k2, then k2 from cn wrapping yarn twice for each st.*

╲⊠⊠ *FC4–Slip 2 sts to cn and hold in front, k2 wrapping yarn twice for each st, then k2 from cn.*

Note: wyib = with yarn in back
wyif = with yarn in front

PATTERN CHARTS

Ribbing (Mult. 9 sts, plus 2–flat knitting; mult. 9 sts–circular knitting)

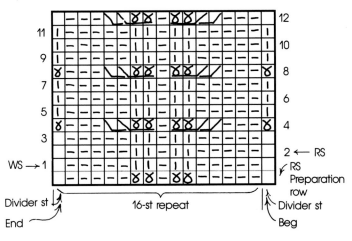

Slipstitch cable

Design with Knitted Cord

Complex-looking textures are a snap with separately knitted cord

by Nicky Epstein

a sweater with intricate cables announces a skillful knitter and often weeks of work. Want the effect but don't have the time—or maybe the patience—for full-blown cables or a similar knit/purl dimensional design? Try my approach: Sew a separately knitted cord to a plain-knit background, applying the cord in any design you like. Knitting the cord is quick and easy, applying it is a snap, and the faux-cable effect you can get, like that in my sweater at left, is as impressive as the real McCoy. This same cord can also be used for striking borders and closures on the edges of an otherwise plain garment.

Stick to smooth yarns for the cord

Knitted cord—generally called "idiot-cord" since it's mindless, repetitive knitting, and more kindly renamed "I-cord" by knitting guru Elizabeth Zimmermann—is easy to make by hand, on a knitting machine, or with a small tool called a cord, or spool, knitter (see "Knitted Cord—How's It Made?" on the facing page). Smooth sport-weight yarns work well for all of these methods. Yarn heavier than worsted weight and bouclé and novelty yarns may be fine for knitting by hand or on a bulky knitting machine but are probably too thick for the cord knitter and will get caught in its needles. (You

Knitted cord offers a shortcut to the drama of cables, as in the cotton sweater at left. Both abstract and realistic images (see the sketches on the facing page) are a breeze with separately knitted cord.

From *Threads* magazine (June 1995) 59:44-47

I-cord designs can be realistic or abstract.

may be able to use a bulky yarn with the cord knitter by anchoring it with even more sinker weights than it comes with—see *Threads* No. 59, p. 20.) Chenille is fine for hand knitting but not for the cord knitter, and it may break on some knitting machines. Whatever your yarn, if you're machine-knitting, adjust the stitch size and use enough sinker weights to hold the knitting taut.

Anything goes for the background— Unlike for the cord, you can use any yarn and pattern stitch for the garment's background fabric. Because I like the cord to be the textural focal point of the garment, I generally use the same yarn for my background and cord, and work a simple background fabric in stockinette, reverse stockinette, seed, or garter stitch. For a cord border or closure at a garment edge, I might work the garment body in a more complex pattern or a different yarn than the cord.

Applying the cord is a snap
It's simple to apply the cord to a background. You need only split a strand of yarn to reduce bulk, thread one of the yarn plies into a tapestry needle, and sew on the separately knitted cord.

I usually sketch the design at the outset of a project, and I use this as a guide when positioning and pinning the cord on the background. Next I loosely baste the cord in place with sewing thread, stitching through the center of the cord. Then, using a single ply of yarn that matches the background, I sew the cord to the back-

ground. I usually sew from the wrong side since it's easier to attach the cord this way. Follow the basting stitches on the wrong side and use an overcast stitch to anchor the cord permanently.

If the design calls for attaching the cord in a curve, I flip the work over at the start of the curve so I can sew from the right side (curved stitching sometimes shows when worked from the wrong side). Working on the right side, I use a simple running stitch to catch the center knit

stitch or two at the base of the cord.

I finish attaching the cord with an anchoring knot and hide the yarn tail in the center of the cord. To hide the yarn tail, I stitch through the cord widthwise, pull the yarn tail out the other side, cut off the excess yarn, and gently tug the cord to pull the tail back into the center. Finally, I remove the basted stitches.

If the design is intricate and has repeated elements, I use a template to make them a consistent size and shape. I find an object of the right size and shape to

Knitted Cord—How's It Made?

Knitted cord is easy to make by hand, by machine, or with a cord, or spool, knitter. The cord produced by these methods is essentially the same but varies in the number of stitches used. A hand- or machine-made cord can be worked with any number of stitches, but I find that three to five stitches makes the best cord in both cases. All cord knitters have either four or six needles (see "Comparing cord knitters," *Threads* No. 59, p. 76) and so produce four- or six-stitch cord.

By hand
There are two quick methods for making cord by hand: I-cord, which makes a completely round cord, and tube

stitch, which creates a flat-backed cord that sits close to the background fabric.
For I-cord: With 2 dpn, cast on 3 or 4 sts. K st, but do not turn. Push st to other end of ndl, and k. Cont knitting sts without turning. Cord will begin to form in 5 or 6 rows.
For tube stitch: Cast on 5 sts. Row 1 and all odd rows: K1, (sl 1 as if to p, k1) 2x. Row 2 and all even rows: (Sl 1, as if to p; p1) 2x, sl 1 as if to p.

By knitting machine
On a single-bed machine, cast on 3 to 5 sts on a bulky machine or 3 to 6 sts on a standard machine. Knit one way and slip st the other way,

using whatever setting is required on your machine to slip.

On a double-bed machine, cast on 3 to 6 sts, depending on the weight of your yarn, and divide the stitches more or less evenly on the front and back bed. Work a cord by alternately knitting rows on the front and then back bed.

By cord, or spool, knitter
There are several brands of cord knitter, but they all work generally the same way. Feed yarn into the knitter, as shown in the tool's instructions, crank the handle, and knitted cord emerges from the bottom of the tool.

use as a template (I used the bottom of a correction-fluid bottle to make consistent loops on the cables on the sweater on p. 74) or make one from cardboard.

To finish the cord ends—I usually knit one long cord and cut it into sections of the length I need. To finish a cut end, pull the cut yarn tail back through the first stitch to stop the raveling, tie on an extra length of yarn to it, thread it onto a needle, and draw it through each live stitch. Then pull the yarn to draw up the end, and secure it with a knot. You can either use the tail to sew the cord to the background (splitting the tail into plies, using one or two to sew with and burying the rest) or bury the tail in the cord's center and attach the cord with a separate length of yarn.

To finish the cord's top end, cut the yarn strand you're knitting with, leaving an ample tail. Then thread the tail into a needle, and complete as for the bottom end.

To seamlessly join the ends of two cords—If you're making a circle, flower, or any motif in which you want to join two cord ends without a seam, cut the cord to the right length, abut the live stitches from both ends, and, using the yarn tail, weave the ends together with a Kitchener stitch (see *Threads* No. 59, p. 18). Finish with an anchoring stitch or two and bury the yarn tail.

When designing, think of the cord as a knitted line

The knitted cord is a flexible line that can take any shape. Your design can be geometric or abstract, as in my sweater on p. 74 and my right-hand sketch on p. 75, or realistic, as in my left-hand sketch on p. 75. The effect depends only on the shapes you make with the lines, although, of course, if you're working with realistic imagery, color, too, plays a role. For example, you'd probably want to use purple or green yarn to make clusters of knitted-cord grapes.

I like to begin a design by sketching the shape of the garment, pillow, or other project, then design the placement of the cording within that shape. Next I choose yarn and colors for the project and *always* swatch to be sure that the yarn and colors produce the effect I want and work with the method I'll use to make the cord.

If you're new to knitted cord or designing knitwear, I suggest that you keep things simple at first by trying out knitted-cord embellishment on small projects like a scarf, hat, or pillow—or even on purchased knitwear (I've also seen knitted-cord embellishment sewn to woven-fabric pillow covers—for this, you should use yarn or thread and a large-eyed embroidery needle).

If you want to start with a sweater,

HOW TO ATTACH KNITTED CORD

Sew straight cord from WS

Basting holds cord in place on RS.

Overcasting with a ply or two from split strand secures cord.

Basting

WS

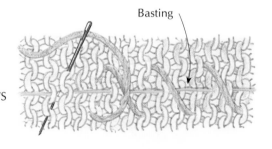

Sew curved cord from RS

Catch center stitches at base of cord with running stitches to secure.

RS

FINISHING THE CORD'S ENDS

To finish cut end

Find yarn tail and pull through last stitch to anchor. Tie extra yarn to tail, thread into tapestry needle, sew through live stitches, draw up, and bury in cord's center.

To finish top end

Pull knitting yarn through last stitch to anchor, thread tail in tapestry needle, sew live stitches off knitting needle, pull up tail, and bury in cord's center.

Illustrations by Phoebe Gaughan

Knitted cord makes unusual borders and closures when applied to or worked into an edge.

choose a classic crew-neck pullover as your first design canvas. You'll find this classic design in numerous knitting books and in almost every yarn company's offering of patterns each season. If the garment presented has a different stitch pattern than you want to use, just use the pattern's measurements and shaping guidelines as the starting point and general template for your design. Make a gauge swatch in the yarn you want to work with to figure out your stitch and row counts.

Add color to the design brew—As you design, think about the effect you want the cord to produce. For the emphasis in your garment to be textural, use the same color yarn for the cord and background. For graphic effects, use contrasting colors for the cord and background.

And remember that the cord itself need not be monochromatic. A variegated yarn produces a beautifully shaded cord like that shown on p. 75. And you can create a striped cord by counting rows as you knit and systematically changing colors at repeated intervals.

Remember, too, that you can combine cords of different colors, twining or braiding them for interesting effects. Look, for example, at the border at center, above.

Makes great borders, closures too
Knitted cord makes a distinctive border for a garment and is a welcome alternative to standard ribbing. The border can be subtle, like the undulating edge on the beige seed-stitched swatch above, or bold, like the yellow and blue hanging-cord fringes above.

Knitted cord likewise makes wonderful closures. Take a look at the two examples at left above, then sit back and dream up your own knitted-cord closures.

Knitted-cord borders and closures are made in one of two ways: They're either knitted separately and sewn to the com-

pleted garment, or they're knitted into a horizontal or vertical edge as the garment itself is worked.

To add cord to a horizontal edge like a hem, knit separately a long cord, cut it into the sections needed, and transfer each section's live stitches to a knitting needle or holder, to be held until needed. Pick up the live stitches of each cord held on the needle or stitch holder at the appropriate spot on the horizontal edge as you cast on this edge of the garment. (For example, pick up 5 sts of cord, cast on 2 sts, and repeat until you have the number of stitches needed for your width.) If your design calls for both ends of the cord to attach to the edge, as in the orange striped border at center above, pick up the live stitches from the cord's other cut end, knot an extra length of yarn to the cut tail, thread the tail, and bury it in the center of the cord.

To add cording to a vertical edge like a front opening, you can either sew it on, as I do (then I don't have to worry about whether the cord's row gauge is compatible with the pattern-stitch row gauge), or knit the I-cord as you knit the sweater. I-cord works well with garter stitch but

with few other stitches because the row gauges are usually incompatible. The following directions are for working a vertical I-cord edge on a garter-stitch sweater: On WS, *Row 1:* K all sts to last 3; with yarn in front, sl 3 as if to purl. *Row 2:* K. Rep 2 rows.

For great effects, just play!
Once you start making and using knitted cord, I bet you'll get hooked. It's such a quick and easy way to create dramatic textures and novel embellishments that it's become a key element of my design tool kit. I like to make lots of cord in various colors and yarns, without necessarily having a particular design in mind. Then I just play with the cords to see what trims and textures emerge. I'm rarely disappointed. You won't be either. □

Nicky Epstein is a nationally known knitwear designer who lives in New York City. Full directions for the sweater on p. 74 are available for $4 from the author at Murrayhill Station, PO Box 317, New York, NY 10156.

KNITTING I-CORD BORDER AND GARMENT TOGETHER

On a vertical edge
Knit I-cord as garment is made.

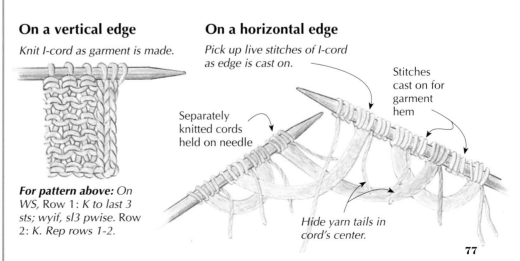

For pattern above: On WS, Row 1: K to last 3 sts; wyif, sl3 pwise. Row 2: K. Rep rows 1-2.

On a horizontal edge
Pick up live stitches of I-cord as edge is cast on.

Separately knitted cords held on needle

Stitches cast on for garment hem

Hide yarn tails in cord's center.

Darts
Add Shape
to Knitted
Garments

Worked vertically or horizontally, darts can dramatically improve fit

by Lily Chin

Vertical darts add smooth waistline shaping to this tailored dress knitted of silk noil, modeled by author Lily Chin. Even the pockets have small darts, so they curve to follow the shape of the body.

Photos by Susan Kahn

even though knits drape and stretch more fluidly than woven fabrics do, there are times when a bit of tailoring improves the fit. When you need to add shape to a garment you're sewing, you fold and stitch the fabric to form darts. When you knit, you can include any darts you want in the fabric *as* you knit it, and get smooth shaping without bulk.

There are two types of knitted-in darts: horizontal darts, which add length to a garment (usually to make room for the bust); and vertical darts, which reduce the garment's width around the body.

Many well-endowed women complain of the dreaded frontal hike-up of their dresses and sweaters. Horizontal bust darts are the answer. Even less well-endowed women like me can benefit from this relatively simple technique, which allows the garment hem to hang evenly, as shown in the photos on p. 81.

You may want to give a garment a more fitted shape that follows the body's contours. Especially for a sweater that will be tucked in or worn under a jacket, you can use darts to eliminate the "spare tire" effect of extra fabric around the waist. If you work all the necessary decreases and increases for darts at the side seams, you'll get an unnaturally sharp waistline shape that doesn't fit correctly. Knitting vertical darts can distribute these decreases and increases evenly around the torso for a smooth fit, as shown on the facing page.

Will the darts show?

Both horizontal and vertical darts may interrupt stitch and color patterns. In solid-color stockinette, seed stitch, ribbing, or other vertical patterns, the short rows knitted for horizontal darts can be almost imperceptible. For patterned knitting, however, especially horizontal stripes or designs in either texture or color, short rows will interrupt the pattern.

A vertical dart will also interrupt some patterns, then restore the pattern when the dart is complete. Either way, a swatch can answer questions about pattern disruption before you begin the darts.

How darts can correct fit

A woman's bust lifts the fabric in front and shortens the lower front edge, as you can see in the top photograph on p. 81. To compensate, the fabric needs to be longer in front than in back.

To allow for this, in sewing, the front is *cut* longer than the back. Excess material is taken away on either side of the full bust in a horizontal bust dart. The side edges, where back meets front, then join

smoothly at the same length. A sewn horizontal side-seam dart removes a wedge-shaped piece of fabric. In knitting, since the fabric is formed and shaped at the same time, you don't see the wedge you're eliminating in the finished fabric. And just as a glass can be half-full or half-empty, a knitted horizontal dart can appear either to take away excess fabric from the sides or to insert extra fabric in the middle of the bodice, as shown in the right-hand drawing on p. 80.

To plan where to place the darts, it helps to chart your body measurements on graph paper, as shown in orange below. It's easier if a friend takes these measurements for you. Whether you're following a knitting pattern or designing your own, sketch the garment schematic over the body outline, lining up the shoulders. For horizontal or vertical darts, you can determine the dart placement by measuring from the bust points.

To plan horizontal bust darts

How much more fabric length do you need to cover the front than the back? To figure this out, mark a line on your body

at a comfortable sweater length with masking tape or a strand of yarn. Standing as straight as possible, drop a tape measure from a central point along the shoulder line down the front, making sure the tape falls over the fullest part of the bust. Record the length from shoulder to marked hemline. Now drop the measuring tape from the same point on the shoulder down the back and record the back length to hemline.

The difference between the front and back lengths is the amount of extra fabric you need to insert to make the garment hang straight all around. This amount will be the depth of each horizontal bust dart. In other words, if the back measures 25 in. long and the front measures 27 in., you'll need to knit a 2-in.-deep bust dart on each side of the front. Once you determine the difference between your front and back, you can simply add this extra amount to any garment front, regardless of length.

If you need the front to be longer by 1 in. or less, you can add it to the garment's lower edge by casting on gradually. First cast on the width between shaping

---

WHERE TO PLACE KNITTED DARTS

Drawing a chart of body measurements makes it easy to determine the correct placement for darts. First measure bust, waist, and hips, then their distance down from the center-back neck. Mark these lengths on graph paper, using 1 square to represent 1 in.

Next, sketch the garment schematic (shown in black) over the body outline. This makes the darts easy to position and allows you to see the extra fabric to remove with a vertical dart.

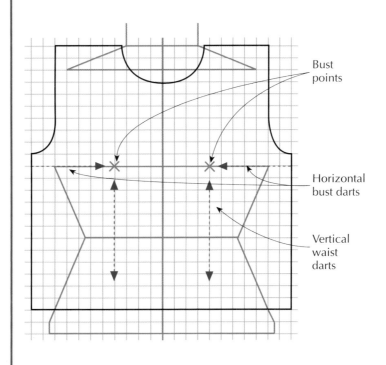

Bust points

Horizontal bust darts

Vertical waist darts

SHORT ROWS SHAPE A HORIZONTAL BUST DART

The flat area at top is the width between bust points (plus 2 to 4 in.) Each line indicates a row to be knitted, and it takes two rows to complete a step (one for leaving left side stitches out of work, and one for right).

Are you adding or taking away fabric?

To create a horizontal bust dart, a sewer removes a wedge of fabric at the side. When you knit dart shaping into a garment, you're actually inserting extra length at the center. The result is the same.

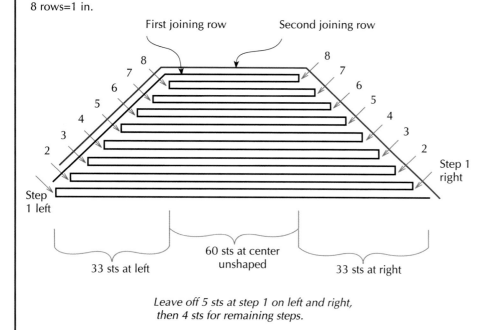

Sample gauge:
6 sts=1 in.
8 rows=1 in.

First joining row   Second joining row

Step 1 left   Step 1 right

33 sts at left   60 sts at center unshaped   33 sts at right

Leave off 5 sts at step 1 on left and right, then 4 sts for remaining steps.

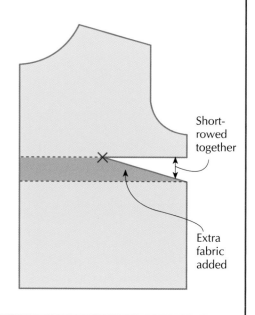

Short-rowed together

Extra fabric added

(the width from bust point to bust point plus 2 to 4 in.). Then, over the course of the next inch of rows, cast on groups of stitches on either side to reach the full width of the garment. Or for a smoother line, cast on the full width and knit the shaping with short rows (see "Shirt-tails for Sweaters," pp. 82-85, and *Threads* No. 56, p. 22).

For more than 1 in. of extra length, you'll insert this length by beginning to work short rows to shape the dart when you reach the bustline. The drawing above illustrates the path of the short rows to knit a pair of horizontal bust darts. It helps to sketch a short-row diagram like this for your garment.

For practice, we're using an imaginary garment with a gauge of six stitches and eight rows per in. in sport-weight yarn. If the garment is 21 in. wide, the bust points are 8 in. apart, and the front is 2 in. longer than the back, then the garment front will have 126 stitches across and require 16 extra rows of length at the bustline.

Use the bust points as a guide for the width of the darts. Shaping should end 1 to 2 in. from the bust point on each side (less for lightweight yarns, more for heavy yarns). The last (shortest) short row is worked over the number of stitches equal to this width, which for our gar-

ment is 60 stitches (8 plus 2 in. multiplied by 6 stitches). By subtracting this number of stitches from the total width and dividing by two, you have the number of stitches to shape on each side, or 33 stitches. These side stitches will be evenly distributed over eight steps formed by 16 short rows.

As a result, at the ends of short rows 1 and 2, you'll leave a group of five stitches unworked; for the balance of the rows, 3 through 16, you'll leave groups of four stitches unworked. The first row after this sequence joins all the short-row steps of one side, and the next row joins all the steps of the other side. These two rows complete the dart, and you can continue knitting normally.

After you join the short rows and work across all the stitches again, you'll see that the extra fabric in the center curves upward to accommodate the bust shape.

To plan vertical darts

In sewing, the area taken away by a vertical dart looks like an elongated diamond shape. In knitting, decreasing stitches from the hip to the waist and increasing to bring them back again later removes the same diamond shape. To distribute the waist shaping evenly around the body, you'll need to knit six vertical

darts: two on the front, generally located near the center of each side below the bust points; two on the back; and one at each side seam, with half the shaping worked on the front and half on the back.

The lower point of a vertical dart usually begins at about the hipbone level. The top of the dart ends 1 to 2 in. below the bust point, again depending on the fabric weight. You can mark the dart length on your measurement chart, as shown in the drawing on p. 79.

To calculate how much to remove for each dart, look at the difference between your hip, waist, and bust measurements. Using our imaginary gauge of six stitches and eight rows per in., suppose the hips measure 38 in. and the waist measures 28 in. If you divide the 10-in. (60-stitch) difference between hips and waist evenly among the six darts, you'll decrease 10 stitches in each dart from hip to waist. To complete the shaping, you'll increase again to reach the bust measurement.

Beginning the darts at the hipbone and ending 1 in. below the bustline, let's suppose the darts need to be 4 in. long or 32 rows from hip to waist, and 5 in. or 40 rows from waist to bust. You'll work ten decreases in 32 rows, which means one decrease every 3.2 rows or two decreases every 6 rows. The increases will occur less frequently: ten stitches in 40 rows means one increase every 4 rows or a pair of increases every 8 rows.

For a fine-gauge yarn, work the decreases and increases in pairs along the length of the dart. For a heavier yarn and smaller numbers to increase and decrease, you can work the shaping individually.

The way you choose to slant your decreases and increases is a decorative decision. If you're knitting them in pairs, you can have one slant right and one left. Or you can work three-in-one decreases and increases into the center stitch. For single shapings, I often knit the right bust and side-seam darts to slant to the right, or away from the center, and reverse the direction for the left side. (For more information on increases and decreases, see *Threads* No. 56, p. 24.)

You can take darts a step further

The methods I'm presenting for working darts, especially vertical ones, are somewhat simplified. In reality, bodies aren't symmetrical. The back is often narrower than the front, and the shoulder blades higher than the bustline. So we could increase and decrease different amounts for the front, back, and side darts, and probably at different rates. For a body with hips that are larger than the bust, we could work a larger number of decreases from hip to waist than increases from waist to bust as long as it didn't disrupt the stitch pattern.

If you want accurate shaping that closely follows the contours of the body, you need to drape a pattern, or start with a sewing pattern that already fits. For such a fitted garment, you'll want to insert both vertical and horizontal darts, giving a shape that resembles a classic fitted sewing pattern. But for all but the most figure-hugging garments, the flexible, forgiving nature of a knit allows you to achieve a flattering fit with identical vertical darts all around the waist.

Many people say that darts aren't necessary in knits. Tell this to a very buxom woman who's never had a sweater hang correctly. Or take a look at the photograph on p. 78 and imagine the same dress with a baggy, unfitted waistline. In a time when many garments are oversized and unconstructed, I find it refreshing to put a little more structure back into my clothes. Instead of "one size fits all," it's "my size fits me." □

Lily Chin designs knitwear in New York City. She teaches knitting workshops nationally and has just completed her second month-long stint teaching clothing design in Kuala Lampur and Bali.

Without a horizontal bust dart, this sweater rides up in front, *creating an uncomfortable tug-of-war for the wearer.*

Giving the same sweater a knitted-in dart produces a smooth, straight hemline *and a comfortable fit for the wearer.*

Shirttails for Sweaters

Here's how to add a modest knit curve to a typical flat hem

by Sally Melville

almost all of the knitting patterns that you see in books and magazines feature square garments with straight bottom edges pulled in by ribbing. But sweaters that have hems that hug the hips are not the most flattering style for many bodies. Curved shirttails are wonderful alternatives; they don't hug our middles, so they can hide a multitude of figure faults. And since they hang freely, they're extremely comfortable, with a carefree and informal feel that is wonderful.

Many hand- or machine-knitting patterns are easily adaptable to a shirttail. Here's the process in a nutshell: You begin by knitting a strip of ribbing that is long enough to go around the front or back curve you want. This strip is longer than one that would fit an ordinary straight edge, but I'll explain how to plan the shape of the curve and how to calculate the number of ribbing stitches that you'll need. The next step is the critical one; this is where you'll transform the straight ribbing into a shirttail. Instead of knitting all the stitches of the ribbing every row, you start the body by working only a portion of the stitches in the center of the row. You'll work back and forth, gradually increasing the number of stitches knitted in each row (this is called *short rowing*, by the way), until all of the ribbing stitches have been brought back into work. Then you can proceed with the sweater as suggested in the original pattern.

For the first shirttail that you try, it's a good idea to keep complications like multiple colors or cables above the completion of the curve, at least until you are comfortable with the shaping.

Garment proportions

The shirttail only works well on a garment that is generously proportioned—long enough and wide enough to swing freely at and below the hips. Plan your front and back widths in one of two ways to make sure the garment is sufficiently larger than your widest measurement: Plan to make the front and back width each at least 2 in. wider than you would make a standard pullover; or check that the total circumference is at least 8 in. larger than your bust measurement or at least 4 in. wider around than your hip measurement. For the most flattering proportions, the finished length should be at least 4 in. longer than the width, with the hem below the hip.

Curve proportions

To plan your own shirttail shaping, you need to understand the nature of the curve itself. My favorite curve for this design is wide and shallow, as you can see in the sweater shown on the facing page. To produce this shape, the base of the curve (the first row you work on the ribbing strip) should be just less than half the sweater's front or back width. For example, if the front width is 100 sts, the base might be 44 sts. Then you divide the remaining stitches in two (for symmetrical sides), and add them in gradual increments until the total stitch count is reached. This curve planning is shown in drawing A on p. 85. It usually works to build the sides of a shallow curve by increasing according to the following general formula: 4 sts once, 3 sts twice, 2 sts three times, and 1 st until all stitches have been increased. This curve would be too flat if it didn't finish with 1 st added at each side 10 to 15 times. If you have too

many or too few stitches to follow my general formula, either enlarge or delete the initial 4-st increase. If you decide you'd prefer a steeper curve, start with fewer base stitches and work narrower increase steps—for example, a sequence such as 3, 3, 3, 2, 2, 2, 1.

A handknit shirttail

All my shirttails have a 1-in. bottom rib (about 6 rows) to prevent the edge from curling. I work it in knit 1, purl 1 because of complications I describe below and because this pattern hangs best. You work the rib as usual on smaller needles. However, it shouldn't be particularly tight. Work a trial swatch to ensure that it is loose enough to hang softly.

As with any other garment, it's easiest to begin with the rib. But you can't just cast on the number of stitches for the body and use them for the rib, because there won't be enough of them to fit around the curve. Obviously, more stitches are needed for the rib than for the sweater body.

Planning the rib—To make a rib that fits around any curve, *you need one stitch for every body stitch, plus one stitch for every time you increase.* In drawing B on p. 85, there are 18 increases per side for a total of 36. Add this number to the number of stitches in the body; this gives the number of stitches needed for the rib—136.

I like to do k1, p1 rib on an uneven number of stitches, with a right-side knit at each edge for neat mattress-stitch seams (see *Threads* No. 42, p. 18), so I'd add one extra stitch—137. You can keep this extra stitch in the body of the garment or decrease it at an edge any time after you've completed the shirttail.

From *Threads* magazine (June 1993) 47:34-37

Planning and knitting a sweater bottom that's curved and doesn't cling is not difficult. You just knit the rib you need, and shape it into a curve with partial rows, as was done for the sweater here.

One small problem still remains before you're ready to begin knitting. If you were to cast on the total number of rib stitches, the rib would flare out around the curve and would not seam well to the adjoining piece, as shown in drawing B on p. 85.

To make the rib taper at the edges, you begin by casting on a few less stitches than the eventual total, then gradually increase at each edge. For a shirttail rib, I increase one stitch at each end of each wrong-side row of ribbing. Therefore, to figure out how many stitches to cast on for the rib, subtract one stitch for each row of rib from the total number of rib stitches—131 stitches.

It works for me to increase at each end of each wrong-side row of rib because my curves are relatively flat and I rib tightly. However, if you rib loosely or are making a steep curve, increase one stitch each end of every row or rib. Cast on the total number of rib stitches minus twice the number of rib rows.

If you work your rib on an uneven number of stitches with right-side knit stitches at each edge, as I do, increase one stitch in from the edge to keep the integrity of the edge stitch for seaming. In other words, after the first increase, the rib would begin and end with two knits. The second increase would be a purl between these two knits, and so on.

Knitting the shirttail—With the smaller (rib) needles, cast on the number of stitches calculated for the rib. Work rib to desired depth, about 1 in., increasing one stitch at each edge on every wrong-side row (or every row if you wish). End with a wrong-side row worked on the larger (body) needles with all the stitches on the left-hand needle. Break the thread, leaving the rib on a needle. ⇨

Photo by Susan Kahn

You now have a long enough piece of rib, but it's not curved. The shirttail of the body must be built into the rib. Begin by slipping rib stitches onto your right-hand needle until you reach the first of the stitches that will form the base of the curve (the center 44 stitches in our example). To figure out how many stitches to slip to get to the base stitches, subtract the base stitches from the total number of stitches on the needle, then divide by 2. Remember to slip the extra stitch for the seam on the right side, if you wish.

Now, using the larger needles, begin the body shirttail shape, which is produced by knitting increasingly longer short rows from the base stitches outward until all the rib stitches have been put back into work: Work a right-side row on the base stitches, turn, slip the first stitch (for a smoother curve without gaps or holes), and work a wrong-side row to the end of the base stitches. Here there will be a perceptible break in the work. Every time you work across the row and come to the place between the stitches just worked and the rib stitches not worked, you'll see this characteristic break.

This is where the short row shaping begins. But you can't simply work the number of stitches in each step of your diagram (4, 3, 3, and so on), because you'll be left with extra rib stitches. Remember, you increased the rib stitches from the number of body stitches by one stitch for every step. Therefore, each time you work in the 4, 3, 2, or 1 sts, you must get rid of that one extra stitch.

You do this by working two stitches together (see *Threads* No. 47, p. 26, for two methods). For example, to bring four rib stitches into work, work three stitches then knit two stitches together. When you reach a one-stitch step, just work two stitches together.

After you've brought all the stitches into work, the shirttail curve is complete and you can proceed with your pattern. Because this shape does not hug the body, the short ribbed band will fall freely. Sometimes the rib has a tendency to flip up. Blocking or washing will usually fix the problem. But for a particularly defiant rib on a shirttail, hang the garment on a hanger and spray the curve with water until it's quite damp. Then pin the front and back rib bands to each other along the lower edge and let the garment hang until it's completely dry.

As you can see, knitting a shape does take some planning. But the same technique used to make a curve can be used to make other shapes as well. Just remember the following principles when you sketch a shape you want: A horizontal line represents a number of stitches. A vertical line represents a number of rows. And a diagonal line is made from a certain number of stitches worked over a number of rows. You're on your way! ☐

Sally Melville lives in Kitchener, ON, Canada, and teaches writing skills at the University of Waterloo. She also teaches advanced knitting and design nationally.

Shirttail shaping on the machine

You can work a shirttail shape on a double- or single-bed knitting machine. But because you can't knit ribbing on a single-bed machine, the methods are slightly different. They also vary slightly from the handknitting technique on the facing page.

On a double-bed machine—cast on for the rib over the total number of stitches needed, minus the number of rows of rib. Work about 1 in. of rib over the usual rib tension, increasing at each end of every other row, as described for hand knitting. Break the thread. Knit several rows with waste yarn and remove the work.

Since the rib has more stitches than the body requires because of the step stitches, you cannot simply transfer all the rib stitches back onto the machine and gradually bring them into work. Therefore, you must rehang the rib stitches on the machine, doubling up stitches at every place where there is a step.

Remove the waste yarn and put all but the base stitches (see drawing A) out of work. Then, with main tension, knit one row on the base stitches. Now you need to work short rows and bring rib stitches gradually into work at each side—in this case by bringing four needles into work at the edges of the next two rows (doubling the last 2 sts to make 1 st of knitting), then three needles into work at the edges of the next four rows, and so on, following the steps shown in drawing C. When all the body stitches have been brought into work, you're ready to complete the piece as desired.

On a single-bed machine—you have two choices. One is to work the rib by hand as in the handknitting instructions. But instead of working the last row on larger needles, finish with several rows of waste yarn on the larger needles. Then hang on the machine and work as for the double-bed instructions. This is the simplest method, but you can't use it if your rib stitches will not stretch to the width of the needles needed; in that case, you will have to use the second method.

You'll work the body, then the ribbing. Knit the body of the garment on the machine first, casting on with waste yarn and ravel cord. Work the body as follows: Put all but the base stitches out of work, and knit one row; now bring the remaining stitches into work as for the double-bed instructions. When the piece has been knitted to the desired total length and removed from the machine, pick up and knit the rib down by hand as follows: With a small (rib-size) needle and no yarn, pick up the number of stitches for the body width—i.e., one stitch for each base stitch and one stitch for each of the 4, 3, 2, or 1 sts increased at each side—but do not knit them in any way (for picking up stitches from waste yarn, see Threads No. 44, p. 16). Remove the ravel cord and waste yarn. With the rib needles, work one row of stockinette or rib, picking up one extra stitch at every step. Now rib these stitches for the desired number of rows, decreasing one stitch at each edge (or one stitch in from the edge) of every wrong-side row. When the rib is the desired length, cast off. —S.M.

Planning and knitting a curved edge

To knit a curved edge with a ribbed trim, you first knit a strip of ribbing and then work the body in progressively longer rows, starting with a short row in the center section of the ribbing. The front and back curves are worked separately. To lie flat, the ribbing must be longer than for a flat-bottom sweater, and it must be tapered where it meets the side seams. The calculations shown are for a sweater pattern that is 100 sts wide in the front and in the back, with a k1, p1 ribbing 6 rows deep.

A. Planning the shape of a curve

To create a shallow curve, plan on using just about half of the body sts (44) for the first row. Half of the remaining sts (28) remain to be brought into work on each side of the curve. The larger increases occur in the initial few rows as shown, resulting in 18 steps per side.

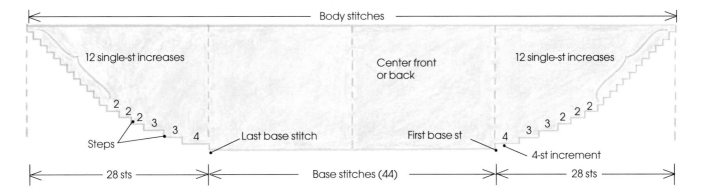

B. Calculating the number of rib stitches

The ribbing cast-on count includes the number of body stitches, extra sts for rounding the curve at each step, and an extra stitch for seaming a k1, p1 rib, minus a st for every row of ribbing to taper the ends of the ribbing at each side seam (drawing, right). Add the tapering stitches back in gradually as you work the ribbing.

Number of body sts =	100
Number of steps =	36
Extra st for seaming =	1
Subtract sts for tapering =	−6
Total rib sts to cast on =	131

Creating a tapered rib

The number of rib sts must increase gradually so the rib is wide enough at the top of the curve, but not too wide at the bottom.

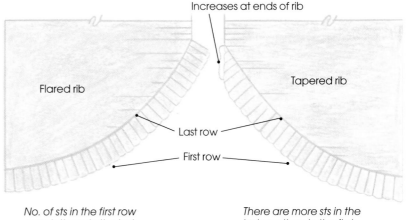

No. of sts in the first row equals those in the last.

There are more sts in the last row than in the first.

C. How to knit short rows for the body on a long strip of ribbing

To reach the first stitch of the base row, slip (sl) rib sts unworked from the left to right needle until you reach the st. Knit the base sts, turn, and sl first st of purl row. Purl base sts and increment-plus-one rib sts: p3, p2 together (p2tog). Turn; sl one st, and k previous sts and increment-plus-one rib sts (k3, k2tog). Continue working back and forth, bringing one increment into work on each row until all sts are in work.

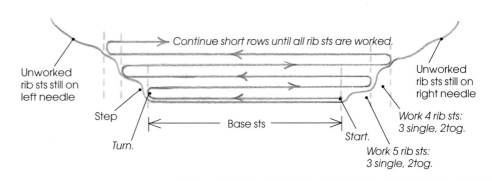

Designing Knitted Hoods

Frame your face with snuggly warmth or sophisticated style

by Deborah Newton

Nestle into your private retreat of soft, furry chenille. Deborah Newton's easy and enjoyable pattern is given on p. 88. (Photo by Yvonne Taylor)

Whether your aim is a cozy refuge from wind and weather or a dramatic statement, a hood can be the ideal topper for your knitted garment. Depending on its shape and construction, the hood can frame and define your face or shelter it in a shadowy, mysterious alcove.

The shape and size of hoods is limitless—from loose, boxy cover-ups to curvaceous tubes that follow the lines of the head and neck. We knitters tend to associate hoods with outerwear or sporty garments where they provide protection from the elements, but a hood is also an ideal accent for a high-fashion design. Recently, I've been admiring soft hoods on drapey, sophisticated designer blouses, and I've often thought that a gossamer lace hood, knitted in a very fine silk, would make a perfect wedding veil.

One of the surprising and delightful things about hoods is that they need not be complex to be attractive. Whether you are a beginning designer/knitter or an experienced one, there is a hood shape to suit your experience. My most recent hooded designs, shown on the facing page and on p. 91, reveal my personal preference for hoods that are a bit cavernous and drape well.

You can find the pattern for the hooded topper opposite on p. 88. It was inspired by a very heavy chenille yarn. A blend of acrylic, wool, alpaca, and nylon, it looks like an enormous, ½-in.-wide, furry pipecleaner. Although the simple fabric that was most appropriate would have been fine with the simplest of hoods, I opted for just a bit of shaping to round the back of the head, avoiding a pointed peak. The thick fabric gives the hood good body, allowing it to stand away from the head slightly.

I tried two hoods before coming up with the luxurious, oversized version I wanted as a focal point for the garment. The extra fabric at the hood edge can be folded outward for a cufflike effect or inward to add body.

Style and design considerations

To design a successful hood, you need to ask yourself a range of questions. First, what size and shape do you want the hood to have? Will it conform to or stand away from the head? If attached, how will it relate to the size and shape of the garment? You'll find some suggestions starting on p. 89. Then think about the knitted fabric. What fiber will best suit both the garment and the hood? What pattern stitches will enhance the design? And, finally, what details, edgings, or accents will make the hood better looking or more wearable?

Although I'll discuss each of these concerns separately, you need to consider them together. For example, when determining the size of your hood, you'll need to assess your fabric's thickness. Thick fabrics require more length and width. Also, the finishing details you choose may alter the size of the hood. For instance, if you're going to have a drawstring, you'll want a little extra fullness around the face.

Fit—Just like a garment, a hood's fit can be close, loose, or oversized (see "Hood measurements" below). A close-fitting hood clings to the head and neck almost like a second skin. A loose-fitting hood skims the head and neck without clinging and has enough ease to allow your hands to enter and hold your head. An oversized hood is designed to stand away from the body with the fabric draping or folding in an interesting way. You can also design a hood that fits the head closely and has a wider, more loose-fitting neckline. Conversely, you may want a looser fit over the head tapering to a close-fitting neck.

Attachment—You can attach a hood to any kind of knitted garment, but it is crucial that the garment fit well without the hood, especially in the neckline and shoulder area. The garment shouldn't hang from or be supported by the hood. And if the body fit is good, a lowered hood won't stretch or weigh down the garment uncomfortably.

You can join a hood to a dropped shoulder garment, but I think a style with better fit in the upper body, such as a raglan or slightly shaped cap sleeve, gives better results. Sloping the shoulders slightly also improves the fit. Always knit the body sections first so you can measure the neck exactly when planning the hood neckline.

I like to make the front neck about ½ in. higher than I would for a regular pullover to position the join of the hood and body at the base of the neck. I usually plan a front neck depth of 2 in. to 2½ in., and I don't often shape the back neck of the body section, especially when I work the hood from live stitches at the neckline.

Neckline width is also important. If a hood is close-fitting, plan a rather close neckline for it to attach to. For the average woman, a back-neck width of six or seven inches is about right for lightweight to medium-weight fabrics. To make close-fitting hoods easier to put on and take off, work a stretchy or ribbed fabric or allow a short placket opening in the neckline area.

A slightly larger hood can be eased, gathered, pleated, or otherwise fitted into a small neckline, but I think loose hoods look best when they emerge from a neckline that is also a bit larger. Aim for a back-neck width of seven to eight inches for light- to medium-weight fabrics. When attaching a large hood, I rarely exceed 8½ in. for the body back neck, unless the fabric is very thick. Generally, the larger the neckline, the poorer the upper body fit.

You can either knit the hood separately and sew it on or knit it into the neckline. For

(Text continues on p. 91)

Hood measurements

For a close-fitting, lightweight hood, these numbers will be close to what you'll use; just add an inch or two for ease. Oversized hoods or those made of thick knitted fabrics will need at least 4 in. of ease, perhaps much more, depending on desired shape.

1. Over the head helps determine length required for hood to go over head and join garment. Measure from forehead over top of head to nape or to neckline. Allow the tape to stand away from your head a bit to simulate the way you'd like the hood to fall.

2. Face circumference is length of hood edge surrounding face; hood depth is roughly half. Measure from base of neck, where hood begins, loosely around face along hairline to same point on other side.

3. Face outline is needed for tubular and turtleneck hoods. Measure as closely or loosely around faceline as desired.

4. Cheek to cheek approximates width needed to go around back of head. Measure from cheekbone, over ear, around back of head, to other cheekbone.

5. Head circumference is necessary for tubular hoods that end in hatlike crown shaping. Measure around head just above eyebrows, parallel to shoulders.

Deborah Newton's Chenille Topper

Knitted in a very thick chenille yarn that produces a soft, furry fabric, this topper is fun, easy, and quick to knit, requiring very little finishing. The edge of this roomy, shaped hood is designed to be folded either in or out for support and accent, and a single large button closes the topper at the base of the neck.

Yarn: Hayfield's "Igloo" (100g = 52 yd.) in color White Owl, #001, from Cascade Yarns [204 Third Ave. S, Seattle, WA 98104; (800) 548-1048]: 14 (15, 16) skeins; approx 720 (760, 810) yds.

To substitute yarns, try doubling or tripling other lighter-weight fuzzy, slubbed, or chenille yarns to produce a fabric of the same gauge and similar weight.

Needles and notions: One pair knitting needles size 13, or size to obtain gauge. One blunt tapestry needle with large eye. One large button, 1¾ in. to 2 in. diam.; one small backer button.

Gauge: To save time, take time to check gauge. In reverse stockinette (rev st st—purl RS, knit WS), 6 sts and 10 rows = 4 in. with size 13 needles.

Measurements: Directions are given for three sizes: Small (medium, large), to fit 32-34 (35-36, 37-38) in. bust. The very thick fabric and oversized fit require you to choose a finished size 8 to 12 in. larger than actual bust measurement.

Working hints: Bind off as loosely as possible to keep edges flat; cast on loosely. Keep edge sts firm, and sew with edges butted to avoid thick seam. To prevent "stairstep" at bound-off edges, slip last st on row before bind-off; slip first 2 sts of bind-off row and pass first over second; bind off other sts normally.

BACK

1. Cast on 32 (35, 38) sts. Leave long tail for seaming.
2. Work rev st st to armhole; end WS row.
3. *Armhole shaping:* Dec 1 st each end of next 3 RS rows—26 (29, 32) sts.
4. Work even to armhole depth; end WS row.
5. *Shoulder and neck shaping:* Bind off 3 (4, 5) sts, work until there are 7 sts on RHN; turn and bind off 3 sts, work to end; turn and bind off rem 4 sts.
6. *Back neck:* Join yarn (RS) and bind off next 6 (7, 8) sts, work to end.
Turn and bind off 3 (4, 5) sts, work to end; turn and bind off 3 sts, work to end; turn and bind off rem 4 sts.

RIGHT FRONT

1. Cast on 19 (21, 23) sts.
2. Work rev st st to armhole; end WS row.
3. *Armhole shaping:* Dec 1 st at end of next 3 RS rows—16 (18, 20) sts.

4. Work even to armhole depth of 8 (8½, 9) in. (work left front ½ in. longer); end WS row.
5. *Buttonhole row:* P2, bind off 3 sts, p to end. Next row: K 11 (13, 15) sts, cast on 3 sts (see *Threads* No. 36, pp. 16-18), k 2 sts. Armhole depth is 8½ (9, 9½) in.
6. *Neck shaping:* From neck edge, bind off 5 (6, 7) sts once; then 2 sts once; then dec 1 st twice—7 (8, 9) sts.
7. Work even to armhole depth; end RS row.
8. *Shoulder shaping:* Bind off 3 (4, 5) sts at beg next WS row, then rem 4 sts next WS row.
9. *Left front:* Work as right front, reversing shaping and omitting buttonhole.

SLEEVE

1. Cast on 18 (20, 20) sts.
2. Work rev st st for 4 rows; end WS row.
3. Next row, inc row (RS): P1, make 1, work to last st, make 1, end p1.
Rep inc row every 6th row for total of 7 (7, 8) incs each side—32 (34, 36) sts.
4. Work even to underarm; end WS row.
5. *Sleeve cap shaping:* Bind off 2 sts at beg next 10 rows. Bind off rem 12 (14, 16) sts very loosely.

HOOD

1. Cast on 46 (48, 50) sts.
2. Work rev st st for 4 rows.
3. Next row, inc row (RS): P1, make 1, work to last st, make 1, end p1.
Rep inc row every 8th row for total of 3 incs each side—52 (54, 56) sts.
4. Work even to 10 in.; end WS row.
5. *First side:* On next row (RS) p 19 sts, slip rem sts to holder. Turn.
Bind off 2 sts beg next 4 WS rows, then bind off rem 11 sts next WS row.
6. *Second side:* Sl center 14 (16, 18) sts to holder. With RS facing, join yarn at hood's other side. Bind off 2 sts beg next 4 RS rows, then bind off rem 11 sts next RS row.
7. *Center section:* With RS facing, sl center 14 (16, 18) sts to needle. Join yarn at beg RS row, then work 6 rows; end WS row.
8. *Center shaping:* Next row (RS): p1, p2tog, work to last 3 sts, p2tog-b, end p1.
Dec 1 st each end every 8th row 3 more times—4 decs each side of center section—6 (8, 10) sts. Work even to length; bind off.

FINISHING

Steam pieces lightly if needed.

Front edge trim: With RS facing, pick up 36 (37, 38) sts evenly along front edge. Bind off loosely in k on next row to keep edge flat. Rep on other front.

Note: To sew, butt edges together with RS facing. Use "baseball stitch" (see *Threads* No. 36, p. 18). Sew body shoulder seams. Sew sleeve caps in armholes. Then sew side and sleeve seams. Sew backed button opposite buttonhole with adequate shank.

Sew center section of hood to inner side sections. Pin seamed edge of hood to neck edge, beginning and ending 1 in. from front neck edges. Sew firmly.

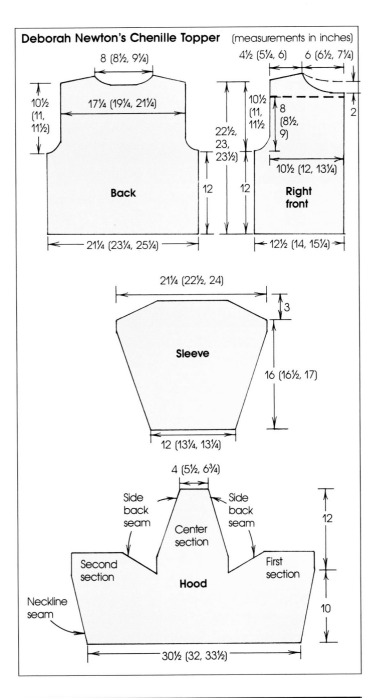

Deborah Newton's Chenille Topper (measurements in inches)

Back

8 (8½, 9¼)

17¼ (19¼, 21¼)

10½ (11, 11½)

22½, 23, 23½

12 | 12

21¼ (23¼, 25¼)

4½ (5¼, 6) | 6 (6½, 7¼)

Right front

10½ (11, 11½)

8 (8½, 9)

2

10½ (12, 13¼)

12½ (14, 15¼)

Sleeve

21¼ (22½, 24)

3

16 (16½, 17)

12 (13¼, 13¼)

Hood

4 (5½, 6¾)

Side back seam · Side back seam

Center section

Second section · First section

Neckline seam

12 · 10

30½ (32, 33½)

MEASUREMENT CHART (in inches)

	Small	Medium	Large
Actual bust	32-34	35-36	37-38
Finished bust at underarm, closed	42½	46½	50½
Length, shoulder to lower edge	22½	23	23½
Length to underarm	12	12	12
Armhole depth	10½	11	11½
Sleeve width at upper arm	21¼	22½	24
Sleeve length to underarm	16	16½	17
Cross shoulder	17¼	19¼	21¼
Back neck width	8	8½	9¼
Face circumference	30½	32	33½

Hood shapes

Hoods fall into three basic categories: Simple boxy hoods, shaped and pieced hoods, and tubular and turtleneck hoods. When you're planning one of these styles, you'll need to refer to the measurements discussed on p. 87, but be aware that each style will require that you adjust them differently. These sketched and schematic versions of each type of hood should give you a general idea of size and shape and a jumping-off place for your own designs. The dimensions I've suggested are based on an average-sized, loose-fitting hood in medium-weight yarn. Although many of my charts indicate seams, you can also work the hoods in one piece by using interior decreases at the "seamlines." Seaming is often desirable, though, to lend structure and support to a larger hood.

Boxy hoods

These are the easiest to make; they're formed of two squares or a large rectangle folded in half, as shown below. They form a peaked point at the center back. You can pick up and knit this hood from the neck edge, or you can work it separately and sew it on. If the neck edge of the hood is larger than the neck edge of the garment, which is usually the case with a boxy hood, it will billow out slightly above the join. Picking up stitches at the neck and ribbing for a few inches will make the neck cling rather than billow where it joins the body. If you're planning a sewn-on hood that will be larger than the garment at the neck edge, ease it in evenly or pleat it at the shoulders.

To make a sharper peaked variation, start by making the neck edge of the hood the same as the neck edge of the body. Work increases on either side of the center-back stitch or stitches until the hood is as wide and as deep as you like; then join the top edges by seaming or grafting.

Simple boxy and peaked hoods

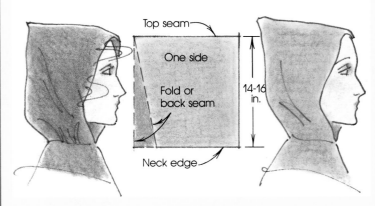

Top seam · One side · Fold or back seam · Neck edge · 14-16 in.

Shaped and pieced hoods

A shaped or pieced hood is essentially a refinement on the boxy hood. Shaping makes it conform to the head more closely, eliminating the peak and rounding the crown, as shown on the next page.

It takes only three pieces to produce an excellent fit. A narrow panel, four to six inches wide, runs down the center back and top of the hood, and curved pieces join it along either side. If the panel is narrow at the back neck and widens toward the face, then the hood will flare at its outer edge. Conversely, narrowing the panel as you approach the face will draw in the hood.

When I make this type of hood in one piece to eliminate

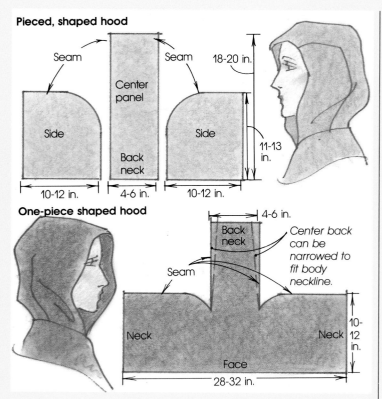

Pieced, shaped hood

Seam · Seam

Center panel

Side

Side

Back neck

18-20 in.

11-13 in.

10-12 in. · 4-6 in. · 10-12 in.

One-piece shaped hood

4-6 in.

Back neck

Center back can be narrowed to fit body neckline.

Seam

Neck

Neck

Face

10-12 in.

28-32 in.

---

attached to the neckline of the garment; a cutout for the face; and, finally, shaping that rounds the hood to fit the top of the head like a hat. There are many possible variations. The turtleneck can be close-fitting and ribbed, which is especially good-looking on a raglan garment; or it can be loose and drapey. The face section can be a simple square, or it can be curved to follow the lines of the face. Or you might make it a mere eye slit. Finally, the top, which should fit like a hat, can be rounded or peaked.

When you're knitting this kind of hood, draw a chart so you can plot the different sections and their measurements. In addition, you should try on the hood in progress to check fit. Make the turtleneck section on the number of stitches used for a

turtleneck collar of the same type, whether it be fitted or loose. Or pick up more stitches, especially if you'll be wearing other garments underneath. When you reach the base of the chin, increase to the number of stitches for the head circumference, plus ease (measurement 5, p. 87). Work even until the point where you'd like to begin the face opening. Bind off this section all at once for a square opening or in steps to shape a curve. Work back and forth until the opening is complete. Then cast on all at once or in steps to form the reciprocal curve. Join and work around even until you near the top of the forehead. Decrease evenly every other round at several points (usually six or eight) to shape the crown. For a pointed top, decrease less rapidly, every third or more rounds.

---

some of the seaming (see the drawing just above and the pattern on p. 89), I usually begin it at the outer, face-framing edge of the hood, working even to the point where the side sections would begin to curve. I then work decreases (k2tog and ssk—see *Threads* No. 36, p. 16; p2tog and p2tog-b are their

counterparts) to shape each side section. Working ssk's before the panel and k2tog's after it will make the decreases lean toward the panel. Since I am working toward the neck edge, I also decrease both sides of the panel to match the hood neck to the body neckline.

Tubular and turtleneck hoods

Tubular and turtleneck hoods range from extremely simple tubes to shapely, almost hatlike hoods that conform to the lines of the neck and the shape of the head, as shown at right. For a pullover, it's best to work the hood on a circular needle to avoid seams. However, if you'd like to join a tubular hood to a cardigan or placket-front garment—or when you're working a face opening—you'll need to work back and forth, at least for the opening.

The simplest tubular hood is just an extra-long tube or turtleneck that can be pulled up over the back of your head. Since the hood is so long, it gathers under your chin for a

cowl-like effect. For a close-fitting tube, use a ribbed fabric; for a softer, drapier tube, knit a smooth fabric like stockinette and allow the edge to roll inside. You can also knit a cone-shaped tube, wider where it joins the body than at the face opening, by decreasing as you work up.

To design this simple tube, decide how large you want the face opening to be. For a stretchy fabric that fits closely, make the opening about two inches smaller than the face outline (measurement 3, p. 87). For a looser fit, allow a few inches more.

The more complex tubular hood has three sections to consider: A turtleneck

---

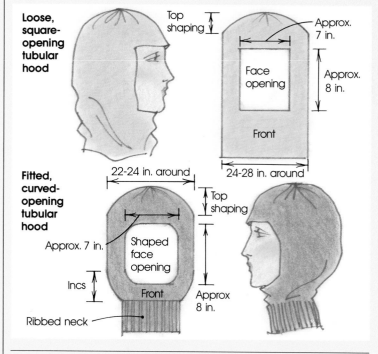

Loose, square-opening tubular hood

Top shaping

Approx. 7 in.

Face opening

Front

24-28 in. around

Fitted, curved-opening tubular hood

22-24 in. around

Approx. 7 in.

Shaped face opening

Incs

Front

Ribbed neck

Top shaping

Approx 8 in.

The sky's the limit

After I'd analyzed and explained the three basic kinds of hoods, I envisioned a different type that I had never tried. The result was a jacket with a shawl-like collar that can also serve as a hood, shown in the photo on the facing page. Unlike conventional hoods, this

drapey one is actually part of the body of the garment, being a shaped extension of the front band/collar assembly. I decided that seed stitch, which doesn't curl, would be a good choice, and I narrowed the garment front edges to allow room for the collar/hood section to be attached. —D.N.

When is a collar not a collar? When it's a hood. Reshape and enlarge a shawl collar to double as a soft hood, as Deborah Newton did here, or choose among the wealth of conventional approaches she describes on pp. 89 and 90. (Photo by Yvonne Taylor)

the greatest comfort and stretch with pullovers, pick up or knit the hood directly from live stitches on the garment. With cardigans or open-front garments, I find that sewing the hood on gives a firmer join, which helps to support the hood's weight, especially when it's worn down.

You can also make a hood that attaches with buttons or another closure. The best way to do this is to work a band at the neckline of both body and hood where they will join. Place buttons on the body band, and buttonholes on the hood band. Although zippers are often used to attach hoods to sewn garments, they're not as successful for knitted ones, unless the fabric is very thick or dense. If you'd like to zip your hood on, choose a very flexible, lightweight zipper to avoid stiffening the neckline.

Fibers and yarns—Since a hood often skims or clings to the skin, it is essential that you choose a comfortable fiber. Rub a skein of the yarn you're considering against your face to see whether it's soft enough. Obviously, fiber choice should also be linked to the purpose of the hood. For a warm hood, choose wool, mohair, or other animal fibers. For a fairly waterproof hood, choose an unscoured wool with greasy lanolin left in the fiber. If the hood is primarily decorative, your choice is virtually limitless, although I would steer away from heavy cottons. Kid mohair is light and airy, and lightweight silk is slick and dressy. If you'd like soft drape as well as warmth, try wool blended with another fiber like rayon, silk, or mohair.

I prefer to work close-fitting hoods in lightweight yarns—sport or, at the heaviest, worsted weight. Larger hoods often have more body if they are worked in heavier yarns. This is not to say that lighter weight yarns can't be used for larger hoods, but they'll tend to drape and slouch. It can be beautiful, if that's what you've planned.

Pattern stitches and trims—The choice of pattern stitches for hoods is as limitless as it is for garments. For design unity, your hood can match your garment; for dramatic or visual interest, it can contrast. If both sides of your hood will show, swatch to find a fabric that looks good on both sides. Many simple knit/purl patterns like ribbing, seed, and block patterns are completely reversible. Another option is to line the hood, but remember to make the outer hood an inch or two larger to accommodate this extra material.

Pattern can also be used to emphasize the shape of the hood. For instance, you might use cables or other panel-type patterns to follow the outer edge or the shaped areas within the hood. You might outline

the seams of a raglan garment with a pattern and continue it up into the hood. Or you could use a different pattern in each section of a pieced hood.

You can knit trim at the outer edge of any hood to add body to the area that frames the face. Larger hoods and those knit of lightweight materials might collapse and look insignificant if they aren't framed in a slightly firmer or thicker fabric. To edge the hood, you might choose a ribbing used in another part of the garment or another contrasting flat pattern. Or you may want to knit in or pick up an unobtrusive hem in plain stockinette stitch. You could also knit extra fabric length for a cuff rather than adding an edging later, as I did on my chenille topper. Or you might work a casing edging through which you can thread a cord to gather the area around the face. A ribbed casing is especially good-looking, as it will close up when the cord is drawn. For sewn-on or picked-up edgings, I tend to use a smaller needle than for the hood itself.

Other hood ideas

For inspiration, consider sewn garments with interesting hoods. You could even buy a sewing pattern with a hood you like to help you plan your knit design.

I often use a few simple sewing techniques to help me check my measurements or to envision and plan a new hood design. To double-check my measurements and experiment with shaping and ease, I drape fabric around my head. Since I have already knit the body, I often use the finished back piece for this purpose. To test a new hood shape, I buy knit yardage of approximately the same weight as my handknit and make a fabric mock-up of the hood so I can check fit and adjust shape before beginning to knit. To plan the hood for the jacket shown at left, I draped, cut, and shaped purchased knit fabric until I had a hood shape I liked. Then I captured it on graph paper to plan my stitch counts.

Don't overlook the fact that hoods can be made and worn separately, unattached to a garment. When you make a separate hood, you'll need to extend, and perhaps widen, the lower edge a bit to cover the shoulders. For a close-fitting hood, a ribbed neckline is a good choice because it will anchor the hood under your chin. For looser hoods, you can plan a scarf or a small capelet to hold the hood in place. Or, the hood can have extensions on the front and back that split at the shoulder like a sandwich board. □

Deborah Newton, author of Designing Knitwear *(The Taunton Press, 1992), is a contributing editor to* Threads.

When Many Yarns Make a Coat

Careful control of tension and floats is key to combining varied types of yarn

by Ann Clarke

When carrying yarn behind a row, weave it in behind every other stitch for a clean finish inside, as in the horizontal bands on this border. When the yarn is knitted in discrete areas rather than carried across the row, use intarsia, as at the top of the photograph.

You need special techniques to make a smooth fabric when knitting a garment that contains a lot of different yarns, from heavy to light. Controlling or eliminating floats plus varying your tension for working different yarn weights can make all the difference.

W hen I knit a garment full of strong images and vivid colors, I can't resist mixing different yarns. Since finding the right color is my primary consideration, I end up with a fabric that contains a wide range of yarn weights in different fibers. As you can imagine, this variety could result in a jumble of holes, puckers, and loose areas. But I've learned to control the yarn as I knit so the result is a smooth, cohesive fabric.

I know this is not the way we were taught to knit, but if you want to combine different yarns, you'll find it's not difficult. By varying the tension to correspond to the yarn weight and by using a variety of knitting techniques from intarsia to stranded weaving in (which I'll explain at right), it's possible to get an even, consistent result. These techniques prevent loose floats on the wrong side and produce a stable fabric.

Many colors, no tangles

I use too many colors in each row to keep any attached to the ball. What a mess that would be! To begin knitting, I cut 3-yd. lengths of the colors in the first few rows, then let the loose yarns hang at the back. But because they still tangle a bit, I suggest avoiding fuzzy yarns, which can gum things up. As you knit, add new colors when needed and continue sections of the same colors by cutting additional lengths of yarn as needed.

To avoid having to finish all these yarn ends later, work them in as you go along. When you add a color, twist in the new yarn behind three stitches before you're going to use it (see *Threads* No. 56, p. 22). And at the end of the yarn piece, twist it behind the next three stitches.

A smooth shift from color to color

The goal is to change colors evenly without holes or accidental show-through from the carried yarns. In a small repeating pattern, such as the border at right, you can carry some colors the length of the row, particularly if the color appears every 10 stitches or less. If the yarn has to span more than 10 stitches, knit with the intarsia method. If the adjacent yarns are very different weights, I sometimes carry a second yarn behind the lighter-weight one to equalize the body of the two sections.

Whenever I carry a yarn, I weave it in behind every other stitch to prevent floats, as shown in the photo at right; this is called *stranded weaving.* Where the yarns are technically too light for the needle size, the woven-in yarn shows through evenly, creating a pleasing flecked color and keeping the body of the knitting consistent.

In an area of small repeating patterns, such as the border of the coat at left, I may have as few as two colors to carry or as many as five or six. If you carry five or six colors over the length of a row, that section is likely to be quite a bit heavier than others. This extra weight can be an advantage at the bottom of a coat because it adds body to the hemline, helping it to hang straight. Nevertheless, when you're carrying many colors, it's a good idea to use a few lighter-weight yarns to lessen the bulk.

When knitting with yarns of varied weights, you also need to pay attention to their overall distribution, which must be fairly even so that the dimensions of the finished piece are not compromised. For example, if the yarns you use at the bottom of the piece are generally lighter than those used at the shoulders, the resulting garment will be larger on top.

If the colors of the lighter-weight yarns are stronger than the others, the intensity of the color may compensate for the slightly smaller stitch appearance. But to produce just a little highlight in a border pattern, a smaller stitch of a light value can add a subtle brightness.

The question of tension

When knitting with a variety of yarn weights, the goal is to maintain a consistent gauge. To achieve a smooth fabric, use more tension with bulkier yarn and a looser tension with the lighter-weight yarns or those with less body. For the medium-weight yarns, use a middle range of tension. At the color changes and where yarns are being woven in, the tension must be particularly consistent so the work doesn't appear lumpy. This sounds difficult, but with even moderate knitting experience, you'll do it quite naturally. This is a technique where too much thought brings trouble. Just give your hands credit for knowing what to do.

Next time you find the right colors in the wrong yarns, I hope you'll consider mixing them. A technique that gives you more knitting freedom and more options can lead to interesting discoveries. □

Ann Clarke, assistant professor of textiles at East Tennessee State University, produces handknit coats and sells them through galleries such as Mobilia in Cambridge, MA.

Index

Look for these and other Threads books at your local bookstore or sewing retailer.

For a catalog of the complete line of Threads books and videos, write to The Taunton Press, P.O. Box 5506, Newtown, CT 06470-5506, or call 1-800-888-8286.